The Old Testament and the Historian

Rox Ambler

2007

The Old Testament and the Historian

by
J. Maxwell Miller

SPCK
London

To My Father

Biblical quotations from the Revised Standard Version of
the Bible, copyrighted 1946, 1952, © 1971, 1973 by
the Division of Christian Education of the National Council
of the Churches of Christ in the U.S.A., are used by
permission.

First published in Great Britain 1976
SPCK
Holy Trinity Church
Marylebone Road
London NW1 4DU

ISBN 0 281 02943 1

Printed in U.S.A.

Contents

Abbreviations

AfOF	*Archiv für Orientforschung*
AJSL	*American Journal of Semitic Languages and Literatures*
ANET	*Ancient Near Eastern Texts Relating to the Old Testament*, ed. J. B. Pritchard (Princeton: Princeton University Press, 1955²)*
ANET Supp.	*The Ancient Near East: Supplementary Texts and Pictures Relating to the Old Testament*, ed. J. B. Pritchard (Princeton: Princeton University Press, 1969)
ARAB	*Ancient Records of Assyria and Babylonia*, ed. D. D. Luckenbill (Chicago: Chicago University Press, 1926–27)
AUSS	*Andrews University Seminary Studies*
BA	*The Biblical Archaeologist*
BASOR	*Bulletin of the American Schools of Oriental Research*
BWANT	*Beiträge zur Wissenschaft vom Alten und Neuen Testament*
BZAW	*Beihefte zur Zeitschrift für die alttestamentliche Wissenschaft*
CTM	*Concordia Theological Monthly*
EvTh	*Evangelische Theologie*
HAT	*Handbuch des Alten Testaments*
HTR	*Harvard Theological Review*
IEJ	*Israel Exploration Journal*
JBL	*Journal of Biblical Literature*
JNES	*Journal of Near Eastern Studies*
JR	*Journal of Religion*
JTUIA	*Journal of the Tel Aviv University Institute of Archaeology*
OA	*Oriens Antiquus*
PEQ	*Palestine Exploration Quarterly*
RB	*Revue Biblique*

RGG	Die Religion in Geschichte und Gegenwart
SBT	Studies in Biblical Theology
ThLZ	Theologische Literaturzeitung
TR	Theologische Rundschau
UF	Ugarit-Forschungen
VT	Vetus Testamentum
VT Supp.	Supplements to Vetus Testamentum
ZAW	Zeitschrift für die alttestamentliche Wissenschaft
ZDPV	Zeitschrift des Deutschen Palästina-Vereins

I

Introduction

THE HISTORIAN AND THE OLD TESTAMENT

When the biblical writers spoke of God they were less inclined to define his attributes in abstract fashion than to describe his concrete acts in history. Thus the Old Testament begins with an extensive survey of Israel's history, Genesis through 2 Kings, which gives primary attention to God's involvement in her affairs. This survey extends in coverage from creation to the Exile. A second survey, 1–2 Chronicles with Ezra and Nehemiah, provides narrative coverage from the time of Saul and David into the post-Exilic period. Together these two surveys account for roughly half of the Old Testament, and the books which comprise them are sometimes referred to as "the historical books."

Literary analysis reveals, to be sure, that both of the surveys are the result of artificial combination of earlier sources. For example, the Genesis–2 Kings survey is based primarily on the "Yahwistic" and "Priestly" sources (Genesis-Numbers with possible elements in Joshua and Judges) and an extensive bloc of "Deuteronomistic" material (Deuteronomy through 2 Kings).[1] But these earlier sources appear also to have been essentially historical surveys. That is, they undertook to recount the significant events of Israel's past in roughly chronological order. The Yahwist began with the paradise scene; described the spread of mankind into the known world, the wanderings of the patriarchs, the Egyptian experience, the Exodus; and may have continued his account to cover the conquest of Canaan. The Deuteronomistic bloc presents such a systematic and carefully constructed account of Israel's history from the conquest of Canaan to the Exile that scholars often refer to it as "the Deuteronomistic history" and to its anonymous compiler(s)

---

1. For a helpful discussion of literary criticism which focuses on the Yahwistic and Priestly sources, see Norman Habel, *Literary Criticism of the Old Testament*, Guides to Biblical Scholarship: Old Testament Series, ed. J. C. Rylaarsdam (Philadelphia: Fortress Press, 1971). The Deuteronomistic bloc will be discussed below in Chapter II.

1

as "the Deuteronomistic historian." Even when we consider the smaller literary units which the Yahwist and the Deuteronomistic historian incorporated into their surveys (lists, songs, narratives, etc.) or explore other portions of the Old Testament, there too we often find a deep awareness of history. The prophets constantly cited in their pronouncements lessons to be learned from history and saw God as active in the political changes of their own times.[2] Historical themes also pervade the psalms.[3]

This historical awareness reflected throughout the Old Testament is enough in itself to warrant the modern historian's attention. But the manner in which the Old Testament writers described their past is also such that it enlivens the historian's imagination and challenges him to apply the most sophisticated tools of his trade. Two characteristics of the biblical accounts deserve mention and illustration in this regard.

First, while the biblical writers gave full attention to matters which were central to their theological interests or which they considered crucial for understanding the past, they hurried quickly over other things which the modern historian would consider important, often giving just enough information to stir the imagination. Consider, for example, the Deuteronomistic historian's treatment of Omri's reign in 1 Kings 16:15–28. The modern historian deduces from this passage and other evidence[4] that Omri's accession to the throne was an important turning point in the history of both Israel and Judah. Omri negotiated an alliance with Jehoshaphat which ended a half century of warfare between the two kingdoms. He restored Israelite control over Moab which had been lost in the meantime, and established the first dynasty in the northern kingdom. Indeed, a hundred years after his death the Assyrians still referred to Israel as "Omri-Land."[5] But the political, military, and diplomatic accomplishments were not what the Deuteronomistic historian deemed important about Omri's reign. What was important in his view was Omri's continuation of the cultic policies which Jeroboam I had initiated, policies which, according to Deuteronomistic perspective, led to the final downfall of the northern kingdom.[6] Omri was not judged to be significantly different from other

2. See H. W. Wolff, "The Understanding of History in the O.T. Prophets," in *Essays on Old Testament Hermeneutics*, ed C. Westermann, trans. and ed. J. L. Mays (Richmond, Va.: John Knox Press, 1963), pp. 336–355; originally published in *EvTh* 20 (1960), 218–235.
3. Cf., esp., Psalms 78, 105, 106, 136.
4. Especially, from the reference to him in the Mesha Inscription (cf. below, pp. 7–8).
5. Sargon II (721–705 B.C.) claims in the annals for his first year: "I conquered and sacked the towns Shinuhtu (and) Samaria, and all 'Omri-Land' (*Bît-Ḫu-um-ri-ia*)." We shall speak further about the Assyrian annals below.
6. 1 Kings 12:25ff; 15:25–26, 30; 16:13, 25–26; etc. . . . 2 Kings 17:7–18.

2

kings of Israel in this regard. All of them apparently followed these policies to some degree. Thus his reign was passed over hurriedly with only a few brief comments.

The very character of these comments, however, suggests to the modern historian that there was much more to be said. Look especially at verses 16:21–22.

Then the people of Israel were divided into two parts; half of the people followed Tibni the son of Ginath, to make him king, and half followed Omri. But the people who followed Omri overcame the people who followed Tibni the son of Ginath; so Tibni died [LXX adds: "and Jehoram his brother at that time"], and Omri became king.

So Tibni died! And his brother Jehoram as well if we follow the Septuagint reading. One must assume from the wording of the text that the death(s) occurred after Omri's party had gained the upper hand, and was in some way contingent upon that fact; yet before or at the same time as Omri's accession to the throne. Was it a natural death? Are we to suppose that Tibni (and perhaps Jehoram) just happened to die at that moment when his followers were "overcome" by those of Omri? How convenient for Omri! Or was there more to be said? Perhaps Tibni was executed, or committed suicide. Josephus suspected the former:

Immediately thereafter the people of Israel were divided into two parties, some wishing Thamanaias (Tibni) to be their king, others, Amarinas (Omri). And, as those who wanted Amarinas to rule were victorious, they killed Thamanaias, and Amarinas became king of all the people. . . .[7]

More recent historians generally conclude that the civil war lasted four years and allow Tibni a more noble death in battle at the end of that period:

There arose then another contender to the throne; namely, Tibni, the son of Ginath, who is otherwise unknown to us. A battle raged for four years in which Tibni received strong support from his brother Jehoram. Finally, both fell together in battle and Omri survived as king.[8]

But few there are who can pass over the incident without giving in to the urge to historical hypothesizing.[9]

A second characteristic which invites closer historical examination of the Old Testament is the fact that the biblical accounts often over-

---

7. *Jewish Antiquities*, VIII. 3 11, trans. H. St. J. Thackeray, *The Loeb Classical Library: Josephus*, vol. V (London: William Heinemann, 1926), pp. 738–739.

8. H. Ewald, *Geschichte des Volkes Israel* (Göttingen, 1866), p. 486. Cf. the similar treatments, e.g., in T. H. Robinson, *A History of Israel*, vol. I (Oxford, 1932), p. 286, and John Bright, *A History of Israel* (Philadelphia: Westminster Press, 1972²), pp. 234–235. The hypothesized civil war which supposedly covered four years is based on the chronological notations in vss. 16:15, 23.

9. Even the present writer could not resist. Cf. "So Tibni died," *VT* 18 (1968), 392–394.

lap in content and occasionally provide what appears to be contradictory historical information. Compare, for example, the parallel reports of Jehoshaphat's unsuccessful shipping venture in 1 Kings 22 and 2 Chronicles 20.

Jehoshaphat made ships of Tarshish to go to Ophir for gold; but they did not go, for the ships were wrecked at Eziongeber. Then Ahaziah the son of Ahab said to Jehoshaphat, "Let my servants go with your servants in the ships," but Jeshoshaphat was not willing.

(1 Kings 22:48–49)

After this Jehoshaphat king of Judah joined with Ahaziah king of Israel, who did wickedly. He joined him in building ships to go to Tarshish, and they built the ships in Ezion-geber. Then Eliezer son of Dodavahu of Mareshah prophesied against Jehoshaphat, saying, "Because you have joined Ahaziah, the LORD will destroy what you have made." And the ships were wrecked and were not able to go to Tarshish.

(2 Chron. 20:35–37)

The theologian will probably pass over this incident as one of minor importance in the overall view of Israel's theological self-understanding. The literary critic will recognize the passages as another example of the complex literary interrelationship between the Deuteronomistic history and the Chronicler's history. But the historian will want to know whether such an incident actually occurred, and if so, which of the two reports is more accurate. Did Ahaziah propose partnership before or after Jehoshaphat undertook the shipping venture? Did Jehoshaphat accept Ahaziah as a partner or not? How did the negotiations between these two kings relate to the earlier alliance which Omri, Ahaziah's grandfather, had sealed with Jehoshaphat? The historian will be curious further about the implications of the incident for Judah's relations with the Phoenician city-states, which otherwise seem to have enjoyed a monopoly on maritime trade in that part of the world, and its implications for Judah's own domestic economy.

NEW EVIDENCE FROM ARCHAEOLOGY

Interest in the Old Testament from an historical perspective has received a boost in modern times, resulting in part from rapid strides in archaeology. Near Eastern archaeology is a relatively recent phenomenon. The first excavations in Mesopotamia were just getting underway in the mid-nineteenth century, for example, and the first systematic excavation of a Palestinian ruin did not begin until 1890 (Sir Flinders Petrie at Tell el-Ḥesi). But archaeologists have been constantly active in the "Bible Lands" since that time. The most active period, as far as actual excavations are concerned, was that between the two world wars. It was also during the post-World War I period that archaeological methodology—stratigraphical, digging, ceramic dating, etc.—reached a significant degree of sophistication.

The artifactual evidence recovered by archaeologists provides the sort of information which rarely can be derived from the written sources: architectural styles, typical ceramic wares, tools, weapons, etc. Such evidence also tends to be more "democratic" than that supplied by the written sources. The latter generally derive from the wealthier and ruling classes and naturally reflect upper class perspectives and concerns. The archaeologist can excavate the poorer sections of an ancient city along with the royal quarter. Finally, with carefully controlled stratigraphical digging and typological analysis of the artifacts, the archaeologist can often discern trends in the life styles of ancient peoples and distinguish the major occupational phases of their cities.

The artifacts are silent, on the other hand, and provide only the most general sort of information, unless interpreted further in the light of written records.[10] For the historian's purpose, therefore, the more significant result of the extensive archaeological explorations in modern times has been the recovery of hundreds of firsthand documents from the ancient Near East. Listed below are some of these ancient Near Eastern documents which have proved to be especially relevant for the study of Israel's history during Old Testament times. The list is by no means exhaustive.[11]

The Amarna Tablets:[12] The first of these clay tablets were discovered in 1887 in the El-Amarna district of Egypt (ca. 90 miles south of Cairo). They are written in Akkadian, a Semitic tongue from Mesopotamia which served as the international language of the Near Eastern peoples especially during the Middle and Late Bronze Ages. Most of them are letters belonging to the correspondence between the Egyptian court during the reigns of Amenophis III and Amenophis IV (Akhenaten), and the vassal rulers of city-states in Syria, Phoenicia, and Palestine. Their chief value to the historian of Old Testament times is that they reflect the political and sociological circumstances in Palestine during the first half of the fourteenth century B.C.—i.e.,

---

10. The relationship between artifactual evidence and written records in historical research will be explored further in Chapter III. Also, a forthcoming volume in the present series will be devoted to archaeology and Old Testament studies. Otherwise, cf. D. W. Thomas, ed., *Archaeology and Old Testament Study* (Oxford: Clarendon Press, 1967); and H. T. Frank, *Bible, Archaeology, and Faith* (Nashville: Abingdon Press, 1971).

11. Especially helpful reference volumes in this regard are: J. B. Pritchard, ed., *Ancient Near Eastern Texts Relating to the Old Testament* and *The Ancient Near East: Supplementary Texts and Pictures Relating to the Old Testament* (Princeton: Princeton University Press, 1955[2] and 1969). Hereafter referred to as *ANET* and *ANET Supp.*

12. J. A. Knudtzon, *Die El-Amarna-Tafeln, Vorderasiatische Bibliothek* 2 (Leipzig, 1907–15); Selections in *ANET*, pp. 483–490.

not long before the emergence of Israel as a nation. We learn from these letters that Egypt's authority in Syria-Palestine was beginning to fade. Some of her vassals were being attracted to the Hittite sphere of influence, or were making local arrangements for their own advantage. Others were pleading for Egyptian aid in the face of attacks by marauding bands. Shuwardata of Hebron and 'Abdu-Heba of Jerusalem identified their attackers as 'apiru.

To the king, my lord, my Sun-god, my pantheon, say: thus Shuwardata, thy servant, servant of the king and the dirt (under) his two feet, the ground (on) which thou dost tread! At the feet of the king, my lord, the Sun-god from heaven, seven times, seven times I fall, both prone and supine.
  Let the king, my lord, learn that the chief of the 'Apiru has risen (in arms) against the lands which the god of the king, my lord, gave me; but I have smitten him. Also let the king, my lord, know that all my brethren have abandoned me, and it is I and 'Abdu-Heba (who) fight against the chief of the 'Apiru. And Zurata, prince of Accho, and Indaruta, prince of Achshaph, it was they (who) hastened with fifty chariots—for I had been robbed (by the 'Apiru)—to my help; but behold, they are fighting against me, so let it be agreeable to the king, my lord, and let him send Yanhamu, and let us make war in earnest, and let the lands of the king, my lord, be restored to their (former) limits![13]

References to the 'apiru in the Amarna tablets have generated much discussion among Old Testament scholars, since this Akkadian term may be related etymologically to the Old Testament designation "Hebrew." It cannot be a matter of simply equating the two, since it appears now that the term 'apiru had fairly wide usage in the ancient Near East, chronologically as well as geographically. But the population of later Israel will probably have included descendants of the 'apiru of the Amarna tablets and others like them, and this may be reflected in the name "Hebrew."[14]

Royal Egyptian Inscriptions: The official Egyptian reports of Asiatic campaigns (in hieroglyphs) and corresponding lists of conquered cities depicted in stereotyped reliefs on temple walls and pylons also provide occasional glimpses of circumstances in Syria-Palestine.[15] The age of Egyptian empire and conquests had already passed by the time

13. *ANET*, p. 487.
14. Although it must be emphasized that the etymological connection between 'apiru and "Hebrew" is by no means certain. For discussions of the issues involved see especially J. Bottéro, *Le problème des Ḫabiru à la 4e, Rencontre Assyriologique Internationale, Cahiers de la Société Asiatique* 12 (Paris, 1954); M. Greenberg, *The Ḫab/piru*, AOS 39 (New Haven: Yale University Press, 1955); Manfred Weippert, *The Settlement of the Israelite Tribes in Palestine*, SBT, Second Series, 21 (Naperville, Ill.: Alec R. Allenson, Inc., 1971), 63–102.
15. J. H. Breasted, *Ancient Records of Egypt* (Chicago: Chicago University Press, 1906–7), esp. vols. 2 and 3 which pertain to the XVIII and XIX dynasties; J. Simons, *Handbook for the Study of Egyptian Topographical Lists Relating to Western Asia* (Leiden: E. J. Brill, 1937); selections in *ANET*, pp. 227–264.

of the settlement of the Hebrew tribes in Palestine, so generally speaking these hieroglyphic documents are only indirectly relevant for the study of Israel's history. The hymn of victory of Merneptah[16] (nineteenth dynasty, ca. 1236–1223), discovered in Thebes in 1896, is an especially interesting exception in that it provides the earliest known non-biblical reference to Israel. The hymn pertains primarily to Merneptah's victory over the Libians, but it concludes with a section in which he claims to have overcome the Asiatics as well.

> The princes are prostrate, saying: "Mercy!"
> Not one raises his head among the Nine Bows.
> Desolation is for Tehenu; Hatti is pacified;
> Plundered is the Canaan with every evil;
> Carried off is Ashkelon; seized upon is Gezer;
> Yanoam is made as that which does not exist;
> Israel is laid waste, his seed is not;
> Hurru is become a widow for Egypt!
> All lands together, they are pacified; . . .

Another significant group of texts, preserved on the walls of the temple of Ramses III (twentieth dynasty, ca. 1198–1166) at Thebes (Medinet Habu), describes that Pharaoh's attempt to protect Egypt from the onslaughts of the "Sea Peoples."[17] The latter were apparently masses of homeless peoples from the Aegean area who moved across the Mediterranean Sea and its coastlands in search of new lands. Among them, referred to specifically in Ramses III's account, were the Philistines (Peleset).

The Mesha Inscription:[18] This stele inscription was erected by Mesha, king of Moab, during the mid-ninth century B.C., and discovered near Dhiban, Jordan, in 1868. It is inscribed in Canaanite, the common language of Syria-Palestine during Old Testament times (to which Moabite, Hebrew, Phoenician, and other Canaanite dialects belong). Mesha erected the stele in connection with a building project at ancient "Dibon," and intended it to stand as a memorial to his reign. Thus he recorded on it his major accomplishments, chief of which was his recovery of Moabite independence from Israel (cf. 2 Kings 3:4ff.). Only the opening lines of the inscription are quoted here:

I (am) Mesha, son of Chemosh-[. . .] king of Moab, the Dibonite. My father reigned over Moab 30 years and I reigned after my father, and I made this high place to Chemosh in Qarhoh . . . because he saved me from

16. *ANET*, pp. 376–378.
17. W. F. Edgerton and J. A. Wilson, *Historical Records of Ramses III, Studies in Ancient Oriental Civilization* 12 (Chicago: Chicago University Press, 1936); selections in *ANET*, pp. 262–263.
18. *ANET*, pp. 320–321.

7

all the kings and caused me to triumph over all my adversaries. As for Omri, king of Israel, he humbled Maob many years [lit., days], for Chemosh was angry at his land. And his son followed him and he also said, "I will humble Moab." In my time he spoke (thus), but I have triumphed over him and over his house, while Israel hath perished for ever! . . .

Several other Canaanite and Aramaic inscriptions dating from the period of the Divided Kingdoms have been discovered as well—e.g., the Siloam Inscription (chiseled on the wall of the entrance to Hezekiah's water tunnel in Jerusalem, discovered in 1880); the Zakir Inscription (discovered at Afis, 25 miles southwest of Aleppo, Syria, in 1904); and the Barhadad Stele (discovered at Aleppo in 1939).[19] Each has its own contribution to make to our understanding of the history of Syria-Palestine during Israel's monarchical period. Except for the Siloam Inscription, however, which is badly damaged, none of them pertains as directly to the history of Israel as does the Mesha Inscription.

Royal Assyrian Inscriptions:[20] The numerous inscriptions of the Assyrian kings are an extremely valuable source of information for the history of Israel because these kings were almost constantly involved in Syro-Palestinian affairs from the mid-ninth century onward. Their inscriptions are basically memorial and/or dedication texts, similar to Mesha's, except that they are written in Akkadian. Often a text will appear in more than one version. Frequently too the body of the text in which the king boasts of his accomplishments will take the form of an annal—i.e., a chronological listing, year by year, of his major deeds.

The value of these annals for the study of Old Testament history is greatly enhanced by the Assyrian practice of *limmu* dating and the recovery of *limmu* (or "eponym") lists. Each Assyrian king presided over the first New Year festival of his reign, but for his remaining years on the throne this honor was passed on to his high officials, each in turn. The official who presided over a particular year was called a *limmu*, and the practice developed of dating events and official documents with references to the presiding *limmu. Limmu* lists were also kept, and enough of these have been recovered to enable Assyriologists to reconstruct the proper sequence of *limmus* from the beginning of the

19. The known Canaanite and Aramaic inscriptions have been collected and published by H. Donner and W. Röllig, *Kanaanäische und Aramäische Inschriften* (Wiesbaden: Otto Harrassowitz, 1962–64). An English translation of the Siloam Inscription is provided in *ANET*, p. 321; and of the Zakir and Barhadad inscriptions in *ANET Supp.*, pp. 219–220 [655–656]).

20. Full English translations in D. D. Luckenbill, *Ancient Records of Assyria and Babylonia* (Chicago: Chicago University Press, 1926–27); hereafter referred to as *ARAB*. Excerpts especially pertinent to the study of Old Testament history in *ANET*, pp. 275–301.

ninth century B.C. to nearly the end of the seventh century B.C.[21] Occasionally these lists refer to natural occurrences, one of which allows for the establishment of an absolute date—i.e., a solar eclipse is recorded for the *limmu* year of Bur-Sagale (tenth year of Ashur-dan III) which can be dated by modern astronomical computation to June 15, 763 B.C. With this fixed point it is possible to establish absolute dates for the remaining *limmu* years and, accordingly, for the Assyrian kings and many of the deeds recorded in their annals. These absolute Assyrian dates serve in turn as fixed points for establishing the chronology of other ancient kingdoms, including Israel.

The Babylonian Chronicles: Various royal records have been recovered from the Babylonian and Persian kings as well. But especially valuable for historical investigation of the last days of Judah and the Exile are the tablets of the Babylonian Chronicles. Combined they cover with only minor gaps the years of the Neo-Babylonian empire. Although actually excavated sometime earlier, they were first published from the British Museum archives in 1923 and 1956.[22] The following entry for the seventh year of Nebuchadnezzar records the fall of Jerusalem in 597 B.C.

In the seventh year, the month of Kislev, the king of Akkad mustered his troops, marched to the Ḫatti-land, and encamped against the city of Judah and on the second day of the month of Adar he seized the city and captured the king. He appointed there a king of his choice [lit. heart], received its heavy tribute and sent (them) to Babylon.

We learn from the biblical account of the incident (2 Kings 24:10–17) that Jehoiachin, who had ascended the throne soon before Jerusalem fell, was carried captive to Babylon. Later his name appears in administrative texts from Babylon which list rations of oil for individuals who were dependent upon the royal household for one reason or another—e.g., as prisoners of war.[23]

Hebrew and Aramaic Ostraca: Most of the ancient documents which have been recovered in modern times derive from Israel's neighbors rather than from the people of Israel themselves. We have already mentioned one exception, however, the Siloam Inscription. Mention should be made as well of the ostraca discoveries. Potsherds served as a handy writing material in ancient times, and potsherds which bear messages (letters, lists, etc.) are referred to as ostraca. These ostraca

21. *ARAB* II, pp. 427–439. Excerpts in *ANET*, p. 274.
22. Cf. esp. D. J. Wiseman, *Chronicles of the Chaldaean Kings (626–556 B.C.) in the British Museum* (London: The British Museum, 1956). Excerpts in *ANET Supp.*, pp. 127–128 [563–564].
23. *ANET*, p. 308.

are often recovered in badly damaged condition. Generally they are written in ink which will have faded through the ages. Even when the contents of an ostracon can be read with some ease, its precise historical context often remains unclear.

Three important groups of Hebrew ostraca have been discovered respectively at Samaria (1910), Lachish (1935, 38), and Tell Arad (1962–67). The Samaria group,[24] approximately sixty in all, are assigned by most scholars to the reign of Jeroboam II and appear to be records of taxes paid in kind—although we cannot be entirely certain of either their date or their purpose. They follow a fairly regular pattern:

> In the tenth year. To Gaddiyahu from Azzo.
> Abibaal, 2; Ahaz, 2; Sheba, 1; Merib-baal, 1.
> (Ostracon No. 2)
> In the tenth year. [From the] vineyard of Yehau-eli.
> A jar of fine oil.
> (Ostracon No. 55)

Most of the twenty-one Lachish ostraca[25] are letters written from a subordinate to the governor of the city. Ostracon IV in particular was probably written just before the Chaldean siege of Lachish (589/8 B.C.). Note the ominous report that the signal fires from Azekah were no longer visible.

May Yahweh cause my lord to hear this very day tidings of good! And now according to everything that my lord hath written, so hath thy servant done; I have written on the door according to all that my lord hath written to me. And with respect to what my lord hath written about the matter of *Beth-haraphid*, there is no one there.

And as for Semachiah, Shemaiah hath taken him and hath brought him up to the city. And as for thy servant, I am not sending anyone thither [today (?), but I will send] tomorrow morning.

And let (my lord) know that we are watching for the signals of Lachish, according to all the indications which my lord hath given, for we cannot see Azekah.

Of the more than two hundred Hebrew and Aramaic ostraca recovered during the excavation at Tell Arad,[26] only a small percentage are sufficiently preserved to be read. Seventeen of these (nine of which can be read quite well) are also official letters dating from the last years

---

24. G. A. Reisner, C. S. Fisher, D. G. Lyon, *Harvard Excavations at Samaria (1908–10)* (Cambridge, Mass.: Harvard University Press, 1924), pp. 227–246. Selected examples, including no. 2 and no. 55 quoted below, in *ANET*, p. 321.
25. H. Torczyner (Tur-Sinai), *Lachish I: The Lachish Letters* (Oxford: Oxford University Press, 1938). Selected examples, including the one quoted below, in *ANET*, pp. 321–322.
26. Y. Aharoni, "Hebrew Ostraca from Tell Arad," *IEJ* 16 (1966), 1–7; "Arad: Its Inscriptions and Temple," *BA* 31 (1968), 2–32. Selected examples, including the one quoted below, in *ANET Supp.* pp. 132–133 [568–569].

of Judah's monarchical period. Nearly all of them are addressed to one Eliashib, apparently the commander of the military garrison at Arad. One of them is especially interesting in that it may refer to the temple in Jerusalem:

> To my Lord Eliashib, may Yahweh grant thy welfare! And (as) of now, give Shemariah half an aroura (of ground) and to Kerosi give a quarter aroura and to the sanctuary (give) what thou didst recommend to me. As for Shallum, he shall stay at the temple of Yahweh.

Aramaic Papyri: Two groups of Aramaic papyri (mostly letters, and legal and administrative documents) provide information of a localized sort regarding Jewish communities during the post-Exilic period. The first group (published in 1906, 1911) dates from the end of the fifth century B.C. and derives from a largely Jewish military colony on Elephantine Island opposite Assuan (Egypt).[27] The second group was discovered only recently (1962–63) in a cave north of Jericho (Mugharet Abu Sinjeh in Wadi Daliyeh) and dates from the mid-fourth century B.C.[28]

Obviously the recovery of so many first-hand documents from Old Testament times has greatly enhanced our understanding of Israel's historical role among the nations of the ancient Near East. But these new sources have also raised a host of new historical questions and sometimes appear to contradict the biblical accounts. We will explore one such example in Chapter II.

THE HISTORIAN'S TASK AND METHODOLOGY

Some comments are in order first, however, regarding the historian's task and methodology. Unfortunately it will not be possible to begin with a handy definition of "history," since the term can mean different things in different contexts. The ancient Greeks, from whom the term derives, used it in reference to "inquiry" of any sort. Today it may refer either to past events in general, or to a reconstruction of these events, usually in roughly chronological order. Contemporary historians find it even more difficult to settle upon a satisfactory definition of their task. Does the historian's responsibility end with his reconstruction of the

---

27. A. H. Sayce and A. E. Cowley, eds., *Aramaic Papyri Discovered at Assuan* (London: Moring, 1906); A. Cowley, ed., *Aramaic Papyri of the Fifth Century B.C.* (Oxford: Clarendon Press, 1923). Selected examples in *ANET*, pp. 222–223, 491–492.

28. F. M. Cross, "The Discovery of the Samaria Papyri," *BA* 26 (1963), 110–121, reprinted in *The Biblical Archaeologist Reader* 3, ed. E. F. Campbell and D. N. Freedman (New York: Doubleday, 1970), pp. 227–239; "Papyri of the Fourth Century B.C. from Dâliyeh," *New Directions in Biblical Archaeology,* ed. D. N. Freedman and J. C. Greenfield (New York: Doubleday, 1971), pp. 45–69.

sequence of past events and his attempted objective analysis of the causal relationships? Or is this only the first step of a task which extends beyond objective controls; the task, namely, of interpreting the past and perhaps even projecting from it into the present and future? Is historical objectivity possible at all? And if not, is critical historical inquiry essentially different in the final analysis from pure speculation?[29]

It can be agreed that the historian focuses his attention on the human past, although note occasional overlapping terminology in the physical sciences—e.g., "historical geology." More specifically, the historian is interested in man's recorded past and deals primarily with the written records. Thus we sometimes refer to that major portion of man's past before the development of writing—more than two million years, depending upon one's assessment of the fossil record—as the "pre-historical" period. This association of the historian's work with written materials admittedly tends to break down when he deals with a situation in which the written materials are scarce and must be supplemented heavily with archaeological data. Actually when the inquiry is based primarily on oral and/or artifactual evidence, we generally refer to the researcher as an anthropologist, archaeologist, or something other than an historian. Moreover, when written sources are utilized alongside (non-written) archaeological findings it is generally the written evidence which provides the framework for interpreting the artifactual data, and not the reverse. This latter procedure has been very much the case in the study of ancient Israel's history, as we shall see below in Chapter III.

Traditionally, historians have focused their attention on political and diplomatic affairs, at least partially because this is the sort of information which often presents itself most obviously in the written sources. But the contemporary historian is very much aware of other factors equally significant in the shaping of the human past—e.g., technological advancements, economics, etc.—even if the information necessary for a proper assessment of these factors is not always readily available. Note also the various specialized branches of historical inquiry which have developed in conjunction with other disciplines: intellectual history, history of warfare, history of art (music, architecture), etc.

The contemporary historian's approach tends to differ from that of his earlier counterparts in three ways: (1) he generally takes a more

29. For fuller discussion of the philosophical and methodological issues relevant to the historian's task, cf. esp. Allan Nevins, *The Gateway to History*, rev. ed. (New York: Doubleday, 1962); Marc Bloch, *The Historian's Craft*, trans. P. Putnam (New York: Random House, 1953); and E. H. Carr, *What Is History* (New York: Alfred A. Knopf, 1962).

critical stance toward his sources; (2) he is inclined to disregard the supernatural or miraculous in his treatment of past events; (3) he is very much aware of his own historicity and, accordingly, of the subjective and tentative character of his own historical conclusions. Let us explore these three points further with specific attention to the Old Testament as an historical source, keeping in mind that exceptions to these tendencies can be cited among historians of ancient as well as modern times.[30]

(1) The ancient and medieval "historian" tended to take the traditions of the past at face value, especially when they referred to the distant past beyond the range of normal memory. He was basically a collector, compiler, and, occasionally, a harmonizer of stories, legends, genealogies, and other traditions. When he introduced his own insights these generally presupposed the essential accuracy of his sources. The modern historian, on the other hand, approaches his sources with the awareness that numerous factors will have influenced their testimony: the philosophical and theological presuppositions of the age in which they were written, their sociological origin and function, the specific intentions which guided their formulation, the particular bias of their author or compiler, and the various changes which may have occurred in their text during the process of transmission from earlier times to the present. Thus he never takes his sources entirely at face value, but carefully analyzes them in order to make proper allowance for the influencing factors.

This analytical (or "critical") approach to ancient texts, which the present-day historian shares with other scholars, is often referred to as "the historical-critical method." Subsumed under the historical-critical method are certain specialized methodologies, four of which

---

30. The cautious skepticism exercised by certain of the Greek historians—e.g., Herodotus and especially Thucydides—should be mentioned here, although the contrast between the supposedly critically minded Greek writers and the more theologically minded biblical writers is, in my opinion, often overstated. Herodotus, after all, was collecting information from "foreigners" about their past, and the fact that he doubted the historical accuracy of some of their more fantastic claims does not mean that he was skeptical of supernaturalism in principle. The biblical writers also rejected much of the mythology of their neighbors. Compare, for example, the Priestly writer's reaction to Babylonian mythology in Gen. 1:1–2:4; 5; 9:1–19. Cf. J. M. Miller, "In the 'Image' and 'Likeness' of God," *JBL* 91 (1972), 289–304; A. S. Kapelrud, "The Mythological Features in Genesis Chapter I and the Author's Intentions," *VT* 24 (1974), 178–186.

The matter of mythology and seemingly incredible stories about the past was not a major problem for Thucydides, since he wrote about a roughly contemporary event in which he himself had participated—i.e., the Peloponnesian wars. Compare in this regard the so-called Throne Succession Narrative incorporated into 2 Sam. 9–20 and 1 Kings 1–2. The latter is an entirely credible account apparently written by someone who had first-hand knowledge of the events described. Cf. Leonhard Rost, *Die Überlieferung von der Thronnachfolge Davids*, BWANT 42 (Stuttgart: Kohlhammer, 1926); G. von Rad, "The Beginnings of Historical Writing in Ancient Israel," *The Form-critical Problem of the Hexateuch and Other Essays* (New York: McGraw-Hill, 1966), pp. 166–204. Cf. also W. den Boer, "Graeco-Roman Historiography in Its Relation to Biblical and Modern Thinking," *History and Theory* 7 (1968), 60–75.

have been treated in earlier volumes of this series and are especially useful to the biblical historian.[31] In summary, they are:

(1) Form Criticism—designed to explore the sociological setting and function of the various literary types (oral as well as written).

(2) Literary (Source and Redaction) Criticism—designed to analyze the larger, usually composite, blocks of material in ancient texts with regard to their authorship, constituent sources, date of composition, intentions, etc.

(3) Tradition History—concerned with the early (usually oral) stages of transmission of ancient literature.

(4) Textual Criticism—concerned with the later transmission of the written texts after they had reached essentially their present form.[32]

Note that the difference between the historian and the form critic, literary critic, textual critic, and others is not that the historian engages in a specialized methodology of his own. On the contrary, he must utilize all of these methodologies from time to time. The difference is that, as he engages in form criticism, literary criticism, textual criticism, etc., he does so with a different purpose. Namely, he is less concerned with the sociological, literary, and transmissional characteristics of the ancient texts as such, than with the implication which these factors might have for assessing the historical testimony of the texts. He wants to reconstruct the events of the past.

As the historian applies the tools of critical analysis to his sources (including the biblical texts), it is not so much a matter of determining *whether* a particular text provides valid historical information, as determining *wherein* the valid information lies. Potentially every document from the past is a useful historical witness, although the valid historical data to be derived from it may not be that which it intends to give. The account of the conquest and settlement of the land of Canaan recorded in the book of Joshua is a case in point. According to this account, the whole land of Canaan was conquered in a relatively short period of time by a unified Israel under the leadership of Joshua (chs. 1–12). The newly conquered territory was divided then among the twelve tribes (chs. 13–21) who were to occupy their indi-

---

31. Cf. also Edgar Krentz's volume in this series entitled *The Historical-Critical Method* (Philadelphia: Fortress Press, 1975) in which he discusses the repercussions of critical-biblical analysis in the ongoing theological discussion.

32. Earlier historians spoke of "lower criticism" and "higher criticism," the former corresponding roughly to "textual criticism" and the latter to "literary criticism." These two terms have fallen into disuse, at least among biblical historians, as the methods for analyzing ancient documents have become more specialized.

14

vidual allotments from that time on (chs. 22–24). A closer examination of the biblical traditions strongly suggests, however, that this is an ideal and oversimplified view of how Israel came to possess the land.[33] Literary-critical analysis reveals further that the book of Joshua belongs to the so-called Deuteronomistic history which, at least in its present form, dates from the Exile—i.e., from some five to six hundred years later than the Hebrew settlement of Canaan, a period in which Israel's possession of the land had become a major theological concern for the very reason that it was no longer an actual historical reality. On the whole, then, the book of Joshua is probably a less reliable witness to the actual historical circumstances of the conquest and settlement of Canaan, than to the interests and concerns of Israel during the Exilic period.

But literary analysis reveals also that the Deuteronomistic history is a highly composite work. That is, while it did not reach its present form until just before or during the Exile and presents Israel's early history in accordance with the idealized and theologically influenced views of that late period, it also incorporates older literary units (songs, lists, narratives, etc.). Each of these "pre-Deuteronomistic" units must be analyzed individually with regard to its own origin and relevance as an historical source apart from its present context in the Deuteronomistic history. Thus, for example, the description of the territorial allotments presented in Joshua 13–19 is based on two sorts of early sources: a series of boundary descriptions which probably date at least in part from the period of the Judges, and a series of city lists. The city list in Josh. 15:20–62; 18:21–28 is especially interesting in that it corresponds to the territory which belonged to the Judean monarchy and divides this territory into twelve districts. Quite likely we have before us here an administrative document from the kingdom of Judah, an invaluable historical source when understood in that context.[34]

(2) That the biblical writers presupposed Yahweh's involvement in human history goes without saying. But perhaps it should be emphasized that they understood this involvement to be, on occasion, direct and overt. They recognized, to be sure, that Yahweh could act indirectly through seemingly normal circumstances in such a fashion that

---

33. Cf. esp. Judges 1.
34. The pioneering investigations of the texts in Joshua 13–19 with regard to their original historical setting and function were by Albrecht Alt. Two of his studies deserve special mention: "Judas Gaue unter Josia" (1925) and "Das System der Stammesgrenzen im Buche Josua" (1927) reprinted in *Kleine Schriften zur Geschichte des Volkes Israel*, 3 vols. (München: Beck'sche Verlagsbuchhandlung, 1953, 1959), vol. 2, pp. 276–288 and vol. 1, pp. 193–202.

his actions would have been noticeable only to the "eyes of faith."[35] But he was believed also to have revealed himself from time to time through "signs and wonders" which astounded believer and unbeliever alike. Consider, for example, the account of the escape from Egypt recorded in Exodus 1–15. According to the account, Yahweh used a miracle to get Moses' attention in the first place, a burning bush which was not consumed. Then he directed Moses' every move as he returned to Egypt and negotiated with the Pharaoh. But according to the account Yahweh also regulated the Pharaoh's decisions, alternatively hardening and softening his heart and thus providing occasion to harass Egypt with one supernatural plague after another. The plagues were followed by two overwhelming disasters: the oldest son in every household died in a single night, and the Egyptian army was drowned by means of an astounding display of divine authority over nature. Why would Yahweh have dealt with Egypt in such a fashion? Were the plagues necessary, since Yahweh controlled Pharaoh's heart and presumably could have arranged for the Hebrew departure without resorting to them? The Yahwist's explanation is entirely logical; namely, Yahweh's purpose was not only to grant the Hebrews freedom, but also to demonstrate his supernatural power over nature and human affairs in a way which would not be ignored.

Then the LORD said to Moses, "Go in to Pharaoh; for I have hardened his heart and the heart of his servants, that I may show these signs of mine among them, and that you may tell in the hearing of your son and your son's son how I made sport of the Egyptians and what signs I have done among them; that you may know that I am the LORD." (Ex. 10:1–2)

This presupposition of the biblical writers that the supernatural and miraculous are significant factors to be taken into account in the understanding and interpretation of history was by no means unique in the ancient world. To be sure, it has been common practice in recent years to contrast Israel's historical views with those of her neighbors on the grounds that her theology emphasized Yahweh's revelatory activity in history, whereas her neighbors associated their gods primarily with the forces of nature. But while there is some truth to this observation, the contrast is easily overdrawn.[36] The fact is that Israel recognized Yahweh as ruler over both nature and human history, and

---

35. E.g., he could use a foreign nation such as Assyria or a foreign king such as Cyrus to do his work without their ever knowing it (Isa. 10:5–11; 45:1–7).

36. Cf. esp. Morton Smith, "The Common Theology of the Ancient Near East," *JBL* 71 (1952), 135–147; R. C. Dentan, ed., *The Idea of History in the Ancient Near East*, AOS 38 (New Haven: Yale University Press, 1955); Bertel Albrektson, *History and the Gods: An Essay on the Idea of Historical Events as Divine Manifestations in the Ancient Near East and in Israel*, Coniectanea Biblica, Old Testament Series 1 (Lund: Gleerup, 1967).

her neighbors made the same claims for their gods. Look again, for example, at the opening lines of the Mesha Inscription quoted above (pp. 7–8). Mesha dedicated the sanctuary (high place) to his god Chemosh because of specific historical accomplishments which he believed Chemosh had granted—i.e., victory over all opposing kings, beginning with Omri of Israel. The theological understanding of history reflected in the inscription is typical of the ancient Near Eastern documents and, except that the reference is to Chemosh rather than to Yahweh, is in keeping with that of the Old Testament.

The frequent references in the ancient texts to divine involvement in human affairs pose a problem for the contemporary historian, especially when the involvement is depicted as direct and overt. The historian of today may not specifically deny the supernatural or miraculous. But it is obvious from the history books which he writes that he disregards overt supernatural activity as a significant cause in history and that he is skeptical of claims regarding supposedly unique historical occurrences which defy normal explanation—i.e., the miraculous. Thus, for example, contemporary historians generally accept without major objection Mesha's claim that Omri conquered Moab, that Israel dominated Moab for some years thereafter, and that Mesha was finally able to throw off the Israelite yoke. Yet they ignore Mesha's insistence that these turns of events were the doings of Chemosh and seek to re-explain them without reference to the supernatural. If Chemosh enters into this "re-explanation" at all, he enters only as an element of Mesha's theology.[37]

Biblical sources receive essentially the same treatment, although some historians are more cautious than others in their sifting out of the supernatural and miraculous elements. Regarding the account of the Hebrew escape at the Red (Reed) Sea, for example, even those historians who are inclined to accept the account as essentially historical and accurate in its present form[38] will, in their own recounting of the incident, tend to emphasize the natural rather than the supernatural aspects of the phenomenon. That is, they generally speak in terms of a low tide and high winds and either suggest that Yahweh worked "indirectly" through these natural phenomena or leave the question of his involvement open altogether. The following quotation from John Bright's *A History of Israel* is typical:

37. Typical are J. Liver, "The Wars of Mesha, King of Moab," *PEQ* 99 (1967), 14–31; and J. M. Miller, "The Moabite Stone as a Memorial Stela," *PEQ* 106 (1974), 9–18.
38. Some historians doubt the account's basic historicity due to its cultic overtones. Others question only the supernatural and miraculous elements, discounting them as folk embellishments which would have occurred quite naturally as the story of the escape was told and retold from one generation to the next in ancient Israel.

17

Concerning those events, to be sure, we can add nothing to what the Bible tells us. It appears that Hebrews, attempting to escape, were pinned between the sea and the Egyptian army and were saved when a wind drove the waters back, allowing them to pass (Ex. 14:21, 27); the pursuing Egyptians, caught by the returning flood, were drowned. If Israel saw in this the hand of God, the historian certainly has no evidence to contradict it![39]

Actually, when the historical-critical method of inquiry is analyzed with regard to its presuppositions, it becomes apparent that more is involved than simple disregard of the supernatural or skepticism regarding miracles. This methodology presupposes, for one thing, that all historical phenomena are subject to "analogous" explanation—i.e., explanation in terms of other similar phenomena. By virtue of his methodology, therefore, the modern historian appears to be presuming in advance that there are no truly miraculous or unique occurrences in history. All can be explained in terms of normal occurrences (low tides, heavy winds, normal folk exaggerations, etc.) without references to the supernatural.[40] The obvious conflict between the biblical claims regarding God's overt and unique actions in Israel's history on the one hand, and the presuppositions of the historical-critical method of inquiry on the other, lies at the heart of much of the present-day theological discussion.[41]

(3) History did not gain status as a separate discipline in the universities until the nineteenth century, at which time much emphasis was placed upon the necessity of writing "objective" history. The historian's task, as it was widely understood at that time, was to probe beneath the presuppositions, biases, and intentions of his sources and to find out "what really happened." The historian's research methods occasionally were compared to those of the scientist; in fact history was sometimes referred to as a science. Contemporary historians are no less concerned with objectivity, but are generally less confident regarding the possibility of achieving complete historical objectivity, and are convinced in any case that the historian's responsibility extends beyond the mere collecting and recounting of cold hard historical facts (if such exist). Surely the historian is more than a chronicler or an anti-

39. Bright, A History of Israel, 2d ed., p. 120.
40. Cf. esp. E. Troeltsch, "Historiography," Encyclopaedia of Religion and Ethics, ed. J. Hastings (Edinburgh: T. & T. Clark, 1913), vol. 6, pp. 716–722.
41. In addition to Krentz, The Historical-Critical Method, cf. Langdon Gilkey, "Cosmology, Ontology, and the Travail of Biblical Language," JR 41 (1961), 194–205; James Barr, "Revelation through History in the Old Testament and in Modern Theology," Interpretation 17 (1963), 193–205; B. S. Childs, Biblical Theology in Crisis (Philadelphia: Westminster Press, 1970); G. F. Hasel, "The Problem of History in Old Testament Theology," AUSS 8 (1970), 23–50; and Van A. Harvey, The Historian and the Believer (New York: Macmillan, 1966).

quarian. It is his responsibility also to understand and to interpret the past.[42]

Actually the historian has no choice but to engage in interpretation. For one thing, the raw historical data associated with any moment or event in time are far too numerous to be reconstructed and recounted in full. If the historian could and did tell it all, his recounting would be endless and unintelligible. Obviously he must be selective; he must focus on the "significant" data and causal relationships. This selective process is itself a form of interpretation. Moreover, it is a process over which the historian does not have complete control, since his possibilities will be limited in advance by the extent and nature of his sources.

Another problem with the "cold hard facts" approach to history is that it does not adequately take into account human factors.[43] After all, if the historian is concerned primarily with the human past, he must not overlook the role which human thinking processes, emotions, objectives, etc. have played in shaping this past. Unfortunately, his critical tools are not always adequate for assessing these human factors. People do not always react the same way in similar circumstances. Their thoughts and actions appear to be generally logical; but the logic does not always begin with the same presupposition and is easily influenced by unpredictable and non-rational emotions. From what perspective, therefore, and on what basis, does the historian interpret *what really happened* in the *human* past? Inevitably, even if unconsciously, he relies on his own experience as a human being. In other words, the historian's conclusions regarding the past will be determined at least partially by the way he himself experiences the present.

This brings us finally to the heart of the third point mentioned above; namely, that the contemporary historian is very much aware, seemingly more so than his predecessors, of his own historicity. He knows very well that his experience of the present, and consequently his understanding of the past, cannot be dissociated entirely from the presuppositions and moods of our times. He is aware, in short, that his historical conclusions and interpretations are themselves located in history, unavoidably subject to historically determined influences, and thus never to be considered absolute.

---

42. The change of mood among historians over the past century regarding historical objectivity and the historian's task is reflected in two especially useful collections of readings: Fritz Stern, ed., *The Varieties of History: From Voltaire to the Present*, rev. ed. (New York: World, 1972); and R. H. Nash, *Ideas of History*, 2 vols. (New York: E. P. Dutton, 1969).
43. Cf. esp. R. G. Collingwood, *The Idea of History* (New York: Oxford University Press, 1956).

II
Interpreting the Written Sources

THE TESTIMONY OF THE SOURCES

We have seen in the preceding chapter that the historian of Old Testament times has two categories of written sources at his disposal. The major source of information relating specifically to Israel is the Old Testament itself, especially the so-called historical books. But the historian also has available, newly recovered in modern times, hundreds of documents from ancient Israel's neighbors. The Old Testament books are composite, including materials of various genres and dating from different periods. Also they have undergone changes during the process of transmission from ancient times to the present. The non-biblical documents are generally firsthand in the sense that we have the originals rather than copies of copies. But they often are fragmentary and/or difficult to interpret linguistically; and they also represent various genres and exhibit overriding intentions which tend to detract from their historical reliability. In both cases, therefore, the biblical historian's research involves careful critical analysis of his sources with attention to their origin, nature, and (especially in the case of the biblical materials) their transmission history. A critical approach to these sources would be necessary even if they did not occasionally conflict with each other.

The purpose of this chapter is to illustrate by means of a specific example the way the historian goes about assessing his sources and the sort of interpretive decisions he is called upon to make. We will focus our attention on Israel's international relations during the reign of the four kings of the Omride dynasty. More specifically, we shall concentrate on Israel's relations with the Aramaean (Syrian) kingdom of Damascus at that time. Our chief sources of information will be the biblical account of the Omride period in 1–2 Kings and the royal inscriptions of Shalmaneser III. Other sources are 2 Chronicles, which makes occasional references to the Omride kings, and the Mesha

Inscription, which has significant bearing on their foreign policy in general. But neither of these latter two sources is quite so important as the former for understanding Omride/Aramaean relations.

1–2 Kings

The 1–2 Kings survey of the period of the Divided Kingdoms gives a considerable amount of attention to the Omride period (1 Kings 16:15–2 Kings 10:27). Most of this attention is focused not on the Omride kings themselves, however, but upon the Yahwistic prophets who were active during their time. We have already noted (see above, pp. 2–3) that Omri's appearance on the scene and his subsequent reign are passed over with only brief comments (1 Kings 16:15–28). He was succeeded on the throne by his son, Ahab (1 Kings 16:29–22:40), and Ahab by his two sons each in turn, Ahaziah (1 Kings 22:51–2 Kings 1:18) and Jehoram (2 Kings 3:1–10:27). One receives the general impression from the books of Kings that the Omrides, especially Ahab and his two sons, were second-rate rulers with regard to both domestic and international affairs. Internally, the kingdom appears to have been torn apart by religious conflict between Yahwism and Baalism, championed respectively by the Yahwistic prophets, especially Elijah and Elisha, and Jezebel, Ahab's Phoenician queen. Externally, the kingdom appears to have been dominated and harassed throughout the Omride period by the Aramaean kings of Damascus.

1 Kings 20:34 implies that Damascus had wrested certain cities from Israel already during Omri's reign. Ahab is credited with two victories over Ben-hadad of Damascus (1 Kings 20). But these were both defensive victories, resulting from battles fought in desperation (cf. especially 20:1–12, 26–27). Moreover, they were only temporary victories. Three years later, when Ahab attempted to recover Israelite territory which still remained in the hands of Damascus, his combined Israelite-Judean army was defeated and Ahab himself killed (1 Kings 22).[1] Thus within two years, first Ahaziah and then Jehoram ascended the throne of Israel under the weight of crushing defeat. The narratives in 2 Kings imply that Syrian armies continued to harass Israel throughout Jehoram's reign. In fact, Jehoram appears to have made every effort to avoid contact with the Syrian forces, even when they probed deep into the heart of Israelite territory (cf. esp. 2 Kings

---

1. Verse 22:1, "For three years Syria and Israel continued without war," refers back to the hostilities described in ch. 20. In the Septuagint, ch. 21 comes before ch. 20 so that the narratives of ch. 20 and 22:1ff. appear in unbroken sequence.

5:1–27; 6:8–23; 6:24–7:20). Only at the very end of Jehoram's reign do we hear of an ill-fated attempt to defend Ramoth-gilead (probably present-day Tell Rāmīth, Jordan) against a new ruler in Damascus named Hazael (2 Kings 8:28ff.).

In sharp contrast to these indications of Aramaean domination and harassment, however, the 1–2 Kings survey credits the Omrides with certain accomplishments which seem to presuppose Israel's national autonomy as well as a significant degree of prosperity. For example, we read in 2 Kings 1:1 that Israel exercised control over Moab throughout Ahab's reign, and in 3:4ff. that Jehoram was capable of mounting a devastating military campaign intended to reassert Israelite authority in the Transjordan. Omride domination of Moab is confirmed, of course, by the Mesha Inscription. Ahab is remembered further for having engaged in an extensive building program, although the narrator refers us for the details to another ancient source which is no longer available:

Now the rest of the acts of Ahab, and all that he did, and the ivory house which he built, and all the cities that he built, are they not written in the Book of the Chronicles of the Kings of Israel? (1 Kings 22:39)

The chronological data supplied in 1–2 Kings for the Omride kings also exhibit apparent conflicts. Note, for example, that two different synchronistic dates[2] are provided for Jehoram's accession to the throne; one which places his accession in the eighteenth year of Jehoshaphat of Judah (2 Kings 3:1), and another which places it in the second year of Jehoshaphat's son, also named Jehoram (2 Kings 1:17).

Shalmaneser's Royal Inscriptions

The Assyrian king Shalmaneser III records military campaigns into Syria-Palestine for the sixth, tenth, eleventh, fourteenth, eighteenth, and twenty-first years of his reign. With the *limmu* lists these campaigns can be dated respectively 853, 849, 848, 845, 841, and 838 B.C. The fullest description of the first of these campaigns is provided by the so-called Monolith Inscription.[3] We learn from it that Shalmaneser was opposed by a coalition of Syro-Palestinian kings in the vicinity of Qarqar (Karkara), a city on the Orontes River belonging to Irhuleni of Hamath.

---

2. The Deuteronomistic history provides a synchronistic date for each of the kings of Israel and Judah which locates the beginning of each reign in relation to that of the contemporary ruler of the other kingdom (1 Kings 15:1, 9, 25, etc.).

3. The Monolith Inscription was discovered at Kurkh (ca. 20 miles south of Diarbekr, Iraq). It is engraved on a stele, along with the figure of Shalmaneser in relief. For a full translation cf. *ARAB*, vol. 1, pp. 211–223. The following excerpt is from *ANET*, pp. 278–279.

I departed from Argana and approached Karkara. I destroyed, tore down and burned down Karkara his [i.e., Irhuleni's] royal residence. He brought along to help him 1,200 chariots, 1,200 cavalrymen, 20,000 foot soldiers of Adad-'idri [i.e., Hadadezer] of Damascus, 700 chariots, 700 cavalrymen, 10,000 foot soldiers of Irhuleni from Hamath, 2,000 chariots, 10,000 foot soldiers of Ahab, the Israelite, 500 soldiers from Que, 1,000 soldiers from Musri, 10 chariots, 10,000 soldiers from Irqanata, 200 soldiers of Matinuba'lu from Arvad, 200 soldiers from Usanata, 30 chariots, 1[0?],000 soldiers of Adunu-ba'lu from Shian, 1,000 camel-[rider]s of Gindibu', from Arabia, [. . .],000 soldiers of Ba'sa, son of Ruhubi, from Ammon—(all together) these were twelve kings. They rose against me [for a] decisive battle. I fought with them with (the support of) the mighty forces of Ashur, which Ashur, my lord, has given to me, and the strong weapons which Nergal, my leader, has presented to me, (and) I did inflict a defeat upon them between the towns Karkara and Gilzau.

The inscription goes on to describe Shalmaneser's supposedly crushing defeat of the twelve-king coalition in further detail. Yet the inscription does not claim that he pushed beyond Qarqar in the direction of Damascus at that time.

The so-called Bull Inscription and the Black Obelisk record Shalmaneser's deeds through his eighteenth and thirty-first years respectively.[4] We learn from them that Shalmaneser was opposed again during his tenth, eleventh, and fourteenth years by Hadadezer and Irhuleni, who were apparently supported by the same coalition. The following entry for the tenth year is from the Bull Inscription. The entries for the eleventh and fourteenth years were worded very similarly, as are the corresponding entries on the Black Obelisk.

At that time Hadadezer of Aram, Irhuleni of Hamath, together with 12 kings of the seacoast, trusted in each other's might and advanced against me, offering battle and combat. I fought with them, I defeated them. Their chariots, their cavalry, their weapons of war, I took from them. To save their lives they fled.[5]

We learn finally from an inscription fragment[6] that Hazael had succeeded Hadadezer to the throne of Damascus and Jehu was already on the throne of Israel by the time Shalmaneser appeared on the Syro-Palestinian scene again in his eighteenth year.[7] There is no mention

4. Both the Bull Inscription and the Black Obelisk were recovered during excavations at the mound of Nimrud, the site of ancient Kalhu (biblical Calah), Shalmaneser's royal residence. The former is inscribed in slightly different versions on two bull colossi (ARAB, vol. 1, pp. 236–241). The latter is inscribed on a squared stele which also bears scenes in relief of Shalmaneser receiving tribute from conquered kings (ARAB, vol. 1, pp. 200–211).

5. ARAB, vol. 1, p. 239. Note that the Black Obelisk does not mention a clash with the coalition during the tenth year (cf. p. 204).

6. Also discovered at Nimrud (ARAB, vol. 1, p. 243; ANET, p. 280).

7. Jehu is depicted among the subjected kings on the Black Obelisk (cf. note 4) with the following caption: "The tribute of Jehu, son of Omri; I received from him silver, gold, a golden saplu-bowl, a golden vase with pointed bottom, golden tumblers, golden buckets, tin, a staff for a king, (and) wooden puruḫtu" (ANET, p. 281).

this time of the coalition of kings which earlier had come to Hadadezer's and Irhuleni's aid. Nor does Hazael receive any such support when Shalmaneser invaded again in his twenty-first year.[8]

The chronological data provided by these inscriptions combined with that recorded in 1–2 Kings seem to require that the sixth year of Shalmaneser's reign corresponded to Ahab's last year. Between this sixth year (853 B.C.), at which time Ahab was among the opposing kings at Qarqar, and Shalmaneser's eighteenth year (841 B.C.), by which time Jehu had already ascended the throne, we must allow for Ahaziah's two-year reign (1 Kings 22:51) and Jehoram's twelve-year reign (2 Kings 3:1). The figures can be reduced somewhat. We need not suppose, for example, that the campaigns recorded for Shalmaneser's sixth and eighteenth years occurred exactly twelve years apart to the very month and day, or that the regnal periods ascribed to Ahaziah and Jehoram were necessarily calculated in terms of full years.[9] But even the minimum requirements of these figures seem to indicate that the battle of Qarqar occurred shortly before Ahab's death and that Jehu ascended to the throne shortly before the campaign recorded for Shalmaneser's eighteenth year. By the same reasoning, Shalmaneser's clashes with the coalition recorded for his tenth, eleventh, and fourteenth years will have to be placed during Jehoram's reign. And the implication of the inscriptions is that the constituency of the coalition remained the same. It would appear, in other words, that Jehoram fought as an ally of Hadadezer of Damascus on at least three occasions.

We have already noted some minor conflicts· in the 1–2 Kings presentation of the Omride period. The following more striking conflicts now emerge: (1) 1 Kings 20 and 22:1–38 describe hostilities between Israel and Damascus during the last years of Ahab's reign, including a battle at Ramoth-gilead in which Ahab met his death. 2 Kings 6:8–23 and 6:24–7:10 presuppose further hostilities between these two kingdoms during Jehoram's reign. Shalmaneser's inscriptions indicate that Israel and Damascus were allies in a desperate struggle with Assyria during Ahab's last years, on the other hand, and imply that the alliance remained intact under Jehoram. (2) The army which Ahab was able to muster for the battle at Aphek (1 Kings 20:26ff.) is depicted as pitifully small in relation to the Syrian army.

In the spring Ben-hadad mustered the Syrians, and went up to Aphek, to fight against Israel. And the people of Israel were mustered, and were pro-

8. Black Obelisk (cf. note 4).
9. Cf. below, note 28 and p. 80.

visioned, and went against them; the people of Israel encamped before them like two little flocks of goats, but the Syrians filled the country. (vss. 20:26–27)

At the battle of Qarqar, however, which must have occurred within the next three years—i.e., before Ahab's death at Ramoth-gilead—his military force was most impressive and by no means inferior to that of the Syrian king. Note, in fact, that Shalmaneser credits Ahab with a larger chariotry (2,000) than all of the other allies of the Syro-Palestinian coalition combined. (3) According to 1 Kings 20:1, 26; 2 Kings 6:24, etc., the king of Damascus who harassed Israel during Ahab's last years and into Jehoram's reign was named Ben-hadad. Shalmaneser speaks of a king named Hadadezer[10] who ruled Damascus at that time.

THE SOURCES CRITICALLY ANALYZED

None of the conflicts observed above is insoluble. All of them can be explained in one way or another without calling into question the essential reliability of the sources. Damascus' harassment of Israel can be seen as an on again/off again thing, for example, with periods of peace between hostilities. This could have allowed the Omrides occasions to undertake building projects in Israel and to pursue imperialistic interests in Moab. Ahab's last years on the throne must be seen as one of the periods of hostility. But one can suppose that Ahab and Ben-hadad laid aside their differences temporarily in order to face their common Assyrian foe at Qarqar, and then, having stopped Shalmaneser's advancement, returned immediately to their own private warfare at Ramoth-gilead. In John Bright's words:

We may suppose that the temporary success at Qarqar had led Ahab to feel that the coalition had served its purpose, or that Ben-hadad's tardiness in fulfilling his promises (cf. chs. 20:34; 22:3) had provoked him to resume hostilities. In any event, he moved to seize the frontier town of Ramoth-gilead, with Jehoshaphat of Judah taking the field at his side; and in the course of the venture he lost his life.[11]

The striking difference between the size of Ahab's army at Aphek and the one he fielded at Qarqar might be explained by placing the battle of Aphek earlier in his reign than 1 Kings 22:1 seems to imply. This would allow reasonable time for military build-up before Qarqar. One suggestion is that 1 Kings 22:2 refers to a visit which Jehoshaphat may have made to Samaria on the occasion of the betrothal of his

---

10. Naturally the Assyrian inscriptions use the Akkadian form of the name, *Adad-'idri*, just as "Ben-hadad" in the Old Testament is an Hebraized form of *Bar-hadad*.
11. Bright, *A History of Israel* (Philadelphia: Westminster Press, 1972²), pp. 243–244. Cf. also M. F. Unger, *Israel and the Aramaeans of Damascus* (London: James Clarke, 1957), pp. 67–69.

son, Jehoram, to Ahab's sister (daughter?), Athaliah.[12] As for the identity of the king of Damascus contemporary with Ahab's last years, it can be argued that the Ben-hadad of 1 Kings 20 had been succeeded on the throne by Hadadezer before the battles of Qarqar and Ramoth-gilead;[13] or that "Ben-hadad" was simply Hadadezer's throne name.[14]

Since the participants in the coalition of Syro-Palestinian kings are never actually identified by name in the inscriptional entries after Shalmaneser's sixth year (i.e., except for Hadadezer and Irhuleni), one need not suppose that Israel continued to support the alliance thereafter. Or, if one concedes that Israel and Damascus did fight as allies on three different occasions during Jehoram's reign, as the inscriptions certainly seem to imply, it can be supposed that these again were only temporary alliances forced on Damascus by the Assyrian threat, and that as soon as the threat had passed each time she returned again to her harassment of Israel.[15] Finally the question of whether Jehoram ascended the throne during Jehoshaphat's eighteenth year or during the second year of his son can be resolved neatly by positing a coregency between Jehoshaphat and his son, beginning in the former's seventeenth year. Jehoshaphat's eighteenth year would, in that case, actually be his son's second year.[16]

Some or even most of these proposed solutions may be correct. But before settling for explanations of this sort it is necessary for the historian to inquire into the reliability of the sources themselves. This means analyzing the documents—both biblical and non-biblical—with the procedures of literary criticism, form criticism, tradition history, and textual criticism. A thorough analysis is not possible here,[17] but the following observations illustrate the far-reaching implications such an analysis might have for the historian's treatment of the Omride/Aramaean issue.

12. J. Morgenstern, "Chronological Data of the Dynasty of Omri," *JBL* 59 (1940), 385–396. Cf. the parallel version of 1 Kings 22:1–38 in 2 Chronicles 18, and 2 Kings 8:18, 26 with 2 Chron. 21:6; 22:2.

13. E.g., D. D. Luckenbill, "Benhadad and Hadadezer," *AJSL* 27 (1911), 267–284; followed by E. G. H. Kraeling, *Aram and Israel* (New York: Columbia University Press, 1918), p. 76.

14. E.g., W. F. Albright, "A Votive Stele Erected by Ben-Hadad I of Damascus to the God Melcarth," *BASOR* 87 (1942), 23–29; followed by M. F. Unger, *Israel*, p. 70, n. 49; and J. Bright, *History of Israel*,[2] p. 239, n. 41.

15. E.g., M. F. Unger, *Israel*, pp. 69–74.

16. E.g., E. R. Thiele, *The Mysterious Numbers of the Hebrew Kings* (Grand Rapids: Eerdmans, 1965²), esp. pp. 196 ff.; "Coregencies and Overlapping Reigns Among the Hebrew Kings," *JBL* 93 (1974), 174–200; S. J. DeVries, "Chronology of the Old Testament," *The Interpreter's Dictionary of the Bible* (New York: Abingdon Press, 1962), vol. A-D, pp. 580–599.

17. I have treated these matters more thoroughly in a series of articles: cf. "The Elisha Cycle and the Accounts of the Omride Wars," *JBL* 85 (1966), 441–454; "The Fall of the House of Ahab," *VT* 17 (1967), 307–324; "Another Look at the Chronology of the Early Divided Monarchy," *JBL* 86 (1967), 276–288; "The Rest of the Acts of Jehoahaz," *ZAW* 80 (1968), 337–342.

Literary (Source and Redaction) Criticism

The books of 1 and 2 Kings are part of a longer survey of Israel's history which extends in coverage from the conquest and settlement of Canaan to the Exile (i.e., the books Joshua through 2 Kings, excluding Ruth).[18] Literary critics often refer to this survey as "The Deuteronomistic History" since it seeks to demonstrate that the theological principles set forth in Deuteronomy were operative throughout Israel's history. Foremost among these was the principle that the nation's well being and prosperity depended upon her fidelity to the Yahwistic covenant. The rebellion of the northern tribes and the establishment of a separate kingdom following Solomon's death, and especially Jeroboam's revival of the cultic shrines at Bethel and Dan, were seen as apostasy. Thus the northern kingdom is depicted as generally decadent and gradually declining until its end with the fall of Samaria in 722 B.C. Consequently, the reigns of all the northern kings are discredited each in turn on the grounds that they ". . . clung to the sin of Jeroboam the son of Nebat, which he made Israel to sin" (1 Kings 15:26; 16:34, etc.). Omri and Ahab receive especially low marks. Omri is said to have done "more evil than all who were before him" (1 Kings 16:25), and regarding Ahab:

. . . as if it had been a light thing for him to walk in the sins of Jeroboam the son of Nebat, he took for wife Jezebel the daughter of Ethbaal king of the Sidonians, and went and served Baal, and worshiped him. He erected an altar for Baal in the house of Baal, which he built in Samaria. And Ahab made an Asherah. Ahab did more to provoke the LORD, the God of Israel, to anger than all the kings of Israel who were before him. (1 Kings 16:31–33)

Obviously it was not in keeping with the theological presuppositions and intentions of the Deuteronomistic history to call attention to the accomplishments of the northern kings, and certainly not of the Omrides. This is not to imply necessarily that the compilers of the Deuteronomistic history consciously distorted the picture.[19] But the theological presuppositions and intentions which guided their work will certainly have influenced to some degree the selection, arrangement, and editing of the material presented. This might explain, for example, why Mesha's rebellion following Ahab's death is recorded, as well as Jehoram's unsuccessful effort to restore Israelite control; but

---

18. Still the most influential treatment of this bloc of material is Martin Noth's *Überlieferungsgeschichtliche Studien* (Tübingen: Max Niemeyer Verlag, 1967³), originally published in 1943. For a survey of other scholarly opinion, cf. A. N. Radjawane, "Das deuteronomistische Geschichtswerk," *TR* 38 (1973), 177–216.

19. As contended, for example, by C. F. Whitley, "The Deuteronomic Presentation of the House of Omri," *VT* 2 (1952), 137–152.

THE OLD TESTAMENT AND THE HISTORIAN

never a word is said, to begin with, about Omri's conquest of Moab. The Deuteronomistic history is a composite work, as we have already noted, which was completed near the end of Judah's monarchical period and/or during the Exile.[20] Occasionally the sources from which its material was derived are identified by name; e.g., "The Book of the Chronicles of the Kings of Israel" is cited in connection with the reign of each of the kings of Israel, and "The Book of the Chronicles of the Kings of Judah" in connection with each of the kings of Judah (1 Kings 14:19, 29, etc.). These sources are no longer available, of course, but it is likely that they were annalistic-like documents based ultimately on royal Israelite and Judean records.[21] The data introduced at the beginning and end of the account of each king's reign—i.e., the chronological data, indications of parentage, and brief notations regarding the king's deeds—were probably derived from these documents.

But the Deuteronomistic survey also includes several cycles of narratives which apparently were derived from other (possibly oral) sources. A relatively large number of these narratives are introduced in the context of the reigns of the Omride kings:

(1) 1 Kings 17–19; 2 Kings 1:2–17—a cycle of narratives appearing in the context of the reigns of Ahab and Ahaziah, and focusing on the deeds of Elijah. A central theme throughout these narratives is the religious conflict between Yahwism and Baalism, championed respectively by Elijah and Jezebel.

(2) 1 Kings 20; 22:1–38—a narrative complex describing three battles between "the king of Israel" and Ben-hadad of Damascus. These narratives also appear in the context of Ahab's reign, and again the Yahwistic prophets play a central role.

(3) 2 Kings 2; 4:1–8:15; 13:14–21—a cycle of narratives focusing upon the miraculous deeds of Elisha. All but the last of these narratives appear in the context of Jehoram's reign, and certain of them (esp. 2 Kings 5; 6:8–23; 6:24–7:10) presuppose a period of Syrian oppression and harassment.

(4) 1 Kings 21; 2 Kings 3:6–27; 9:1–10:27—three other narratives which involve the Omride kings and Yahwistic prophets (Elijah and Elisha) but do not belong to either of the above groups.

Note that the evidence of Aramaean hostilities toward Israel during the Omride period derives entirely from the second and third of these narrative groups. The battle accounts in 1 Kings 20 and 22:1–38 contain

---

20. Apparently more than one stage of Deuteronomistic compilation and/or redaction was involved. How early that process of Deuteronomistic editing began is open to question.

21. Some scholars contend that only one such source was involved which the Deuteronomistic compilers called by two different names. For fuller discussion of the issues involved cf. S. R. Bin-Nun, "Formulas from Royal Records of Israel and of Juda," VT 18 (1968), 414–432.

our only indication of hostilities during Ahab's reign. Certain of the Elisha narratives are our sole indication of hostilities during Jehoram's reign. Otherwise we read only of the clash between Hazael and Jehoram at the very end of the latter's reign—i.e., the clash which occasioned Jehoram's death and the end of the Omride dynasty (2 Kings 8:28ff.)—and continued Syrian harassment during the following period of the Jehu dynasty (2 Kings 10:32–33; 13:3–5, 7, 22–25).

Form Criticism

The "Monolith Inscription," the "Bull Inscriptions," and the "Black Obelisk" belong to a specific genre of ancient Near Eastern literature which perhaps can best be labeled "memorial inscriptions."[22] The inscriptions of this genre were normally inscribed in public places during the reign of the king whose deeds they proclaim, their purpose being to magnify his prestige and to provide a record of his accomplishments for his own and later generations. There is considerable variety within the genre, depending for one thing upon the circumstances which occasioned each particular inscription. But generally the memorial inscriptions of the Syro-Palestinian and Mesopotamian kings reflect the following threefold structure:

(1) An introductory statement which identifies the king, indicates his royal credentials, and claims divine support for his reign.

(2) A review of the king's major accomplishments, or an accounting of the particular accomplishment which occasioned the inscription. Often the Mesopotamian kings listed their deeds in annalistic fashion —i.e., arranged chronologically, year by year.

(3) A curse upon anyone who removed the inscription or damaged it in any way. This third element is less constant and is not represented in the three inscriptions under discussion.

In accordance with their intention, these inscriptions tend to report only matters which enhance the king's fame and prestige, or which can be made to appear in his favor. Exaggeration and excessive claims are the order of the day. In the Monolith Inscription, for example, which was composed within a year after the battle of Qarqar,[23] Shalmaneser claims to have slain fourteen thousand of the enemy on that occasion. This was probably an exaggeration to begin with; but some years later, when the same battle is reported again in the Bull Inscription, the death count has risen to twenty-five thousand. Even

22. Cf. S. Mowinckel, "Die vorderasiatischen Königs— und Fürsteninschriften. Eine stilistische Studie," *Eucharisterion*, ed. Hans Schmidt (Göttingen, 1923), pp. 278–321; and Miller, "The Moabite Stone as a Memorial Stela," *PEQ* 106 (1974).

23. Since this inscription records deeds for only the first six years of Shalmaneser's reign, we can be relatively certain that it was composed during or soon after the end of his sixth year.

Shalmaneser's claim of decisive victory at Qarqar is probably an over-statement. If the victory was as overwhelming as he reports, why is he so uncharacteristically silent in the inscriptions regarding the spoils of the victory (except for captured military hardware)? And why did he not push farther into the territory of the defeated kings which supposedly lay open to him?

In spite of their exaggerations, however, the memorial inscriptions are generally free of miraculous and superhuman claims. This is due in part, of course, to the fact that they were composed and displayed publicly soon after the events described. The king's contemporaries, who were already familiar with his failures as well as his successes, could be expected to go along with a certain amount of exaggeration. But utterly fantastic or superhuman claims would never have been taken seriously.

Finally, the memorial inscriptions are cast in highly stylized and formulaic language. Compare, for example, the entries in Shalmaneser's inscriptions regarding his supposedly overwhelming victories over the Syro-Palestinian coalition during his eleventh and fourteenth years with the entry quoted above (p. 23) for his tenth year.

Bull Inscription
In my eleventh year of reign I departed from Nineveh. The ninth time I crossed the Euphrates at its flood. . . .

At that time Hadad-ezer of Aram, Irhuleni of Hamath, together with 12 kings of the seacoast, trusted in each other's might and advanced against me, offering battle and combat. I fought with them, I defeated them. 10,000 of their warriors I slew with the sword. Their chariots, their cavalry, their weapons of war I took from them.

. . . .

In my fourteenth year of reign I mustered (the people) of the whole wide land, in countless numbers, with 120,000 of my soldiers I crossed the Euphrates at its flood. . . .

At that time Hadad-ezer of Aram, Irhuleni of Hamath, together with 12 kings of the seacoast, the upper and the lower, mustered their numerous armies, of countless numbers, (and) advanced against me: I battled with them. I defeated them. Their chariots, their cavalry, I destroyed, their weapons of war I took from them. To save their lives they fled.

Black Obelisk
In my eleventh year of reign I crossed the Euphrates for the ninth time. . . .

Against the cities of the land of Hamath, I descended. 89 cities I captured. Hadad-ezer of Aram [?Damascus] (and) twelve kings of the land of Hatti stood by each other. I accomplished their overthrow.

. . . .

In my fourteenth year of reign I mustered (all the resources of my) land. I crossed the Euphrates. Twelve kings advanced to meet me. I battled with them. I accomplished their overthrow.

The entries for all three of these victories are cast in the same stylized wording and with few significant details. They are, in short, formulaic victory reports. The historian would be unwise to draw any more specific conclusions from them than that Shalmaneser campaigned in northern Syria during the years indicated and that he met with some opposition.

The narratives of the Elijah and Elisha cycles (1 Kings 17–19; 2 Kings 1:2–17; 2; 4:1–8:15; 13:14–21) are typical of another literary genre, "prophetic narratives," which differ from the memorial inscriptions in almost every respect. Whereas the memorial inscriptions were official documents displayed publicly already during the reigns of the kings whose deeds they proclaimed, the prophetic narratives emerged gradually from the population at large and were transmitted orally for a period of time before having been reduced to writing. Instead of the prescribed structure and formulaic language of the inscriptions, the prophetic narratives are generally short, self-contained stories rendered in simple prose. The inscriptions were designed to magnify the king's prestige. The prophetic narratives seek to glorify the prophets, often at the expense of the king. The inscriptions tend to exaggerate, but remain roughly within the realm of normal human experience. The prophetic narratives reflect a lively folk imagination and are strongly inclined toward the miraculous. The inscriptions deal mainly with matters of national and international significance—military victories, public building projects, etc.; the prophetic narratives are often concerned with private affairs—a poor widow and her creditors (2 Kings 4:1–7), a wealthy woman who was barren (4:8–37), a Syrian commander who had leprosy (5:1–27).

When the prophetic narratives do occasionally allude to national or international circumstances, they generally do so only vaguely. Consider, for example, the Elisha story in 2 Kings 6:8–23. The story is set against a background of Israelite-Aramaean hostilities, but the reader will learn little about the political circumstances of these hostilities from the story itself. It begins, for all practical purposes, "once upon a time." The kings involved are not even identified by name.

Once when the king of Syria was warring against Israel, he took counsel with his servants, saying, "At such and such a place shall be my camp." But the man of God sent word to the king of Israel, "Beware that you do not pass this place, for the Syrians are going down there." And the king of Israel sent to the place of which the man of God told him. Thus he used to warn him, so that he saved himself there more than once or twice. (vss. 8–10)

In fact, the anonymity of the king(s) of Israel who appear in the

31

Elisha narratives is one of the notable characteristics of the Elisha cycle. The reference to Joash by name in 2 Kings 13:14 is the single exception. And even this identification, as we shall see below, was probably made secondarily when the story was incorporated into the Deuteronomistic history. Actually Ben-hadad of Damascus is a less anonymous figure in the Elisha cycle than the king(s) of Israel, probably due to his role in these stories as Elisha's chief adversary.

The anonymity of the king(s) of Israel in the Elisha stories further complicates the issue of Israelite/Aramaean relations during the Omride period. We noted above that these stories are our only evidence for hostilities between the two kingdoms during Jehoram's reign—i.e., before Hazael's attack upon Ramoth-gilead just before Jehoram's death (2 Kings 8:28f.). Actually it is not the stories themselves which provide the evidence, since they never actually identify the king(s) of Israel to whose reign(s) they pertain. The evidence consists, rather, of the fact that when these stories were incorporated into the Deuteronomistic history they were placed in the context of Jehoram's reign. The compilers of the Deuteronomistic history placed them there for a quite logical reason which will become apparent below. But at least three factors strongly suggest that they might have been associated more accurately with the reigns of the first three kings of the (later) Jehu dynasty (Jehu, Jehoahaz, and Joash; 2 Kings 9:1ff.):

(1) These narratives presuppose a supportive relationship between Elisha and "the king of Israel." This is out of keeping with the indications otherwise that the Yahwistic prophets in general and Elisha in particular strongly opposed the Omride kings (cf. especially 2 Kings 3:13ff.). Yet it is precisely what we would expect if the king(s) involved in these stories were members of the Jehu dynasty. According to 2 Kings 9:1ff., Elisha initiated the coup which brought the Jehu dynasty to power.

(2) We have already noted that the biblical texts are otherwise silent regarding Aramaean hostilities during Jehoram's reign, but that they clearly indicate a period of Syrian oppression beginning with Hazael's attack upon Ramoth-gilead at the very end of Jehoram's reign and reaching a peak during the reigns of Jehu, Jehoahaz, and Joash (2 Kings 8:28f.; 10:32–33; 13:3–5, 7, 22–25). Obviously the Elisha narratives, which presuppose a period of Syrian oppression, would fit better in this latter context.

(3) The positioning of the Elisha narratives in the context of Jehoram's reign forces the conclusion that the Ben-hadad who appears in them preceded Hazael to the throne (cf. esp. 2 Kings 6:24 and

8:7–15). Shalmaneser's inscriptions identify Hazael's predecessor as Hadadezer, however, and the compilers of the Deuteronomistic history themselves associated the last of the Elisha stories (2 Kings 13:19–21) with events which occurred during the reigns of Joash and of Hazael's son *who was named Ben-hadad* (2 Kings 13:3, 24).

Tradition History

The narratives incorporated into the 1–2 Kings account of the Omride period already had a long and complicated "pre-Deuteron-omistic" transmission history. Occasionally it is possible to trace the early stages of this transmission, at least in broad outline, and to discern changes which occurred during the process.[24] For example, the transmission history of the accounts of the "king of Israel's" three battles with Ben-hadad in 1 Kings 20 and 22:1–38 must have been roughly as follows.

(1) These narratives appear to have originated in the northern kingdom as reports of three battles between Israel and Damascus: one fought in defense of Samaria, another soon after at Aphek, and then a third approximately three years later at Ramoth-gilead.

(2) Later these accounts apparently were taken over and transmitted within circles which were less interested in political and military matters than in the role of the prophets in Israel's history. Accordingly, during the process of telling and retelling within these prophetically oriented circles, they were gradually revised and expanded in such a fashion as to shift the focus of attention to the prophets. The kings involved in the battles were allowed to fade into the background and finally reduced to anonymity.[25] In short, these accounts were transformed into "prophetic narratives."

(3) After the fall of the northern kingdom the narratives were preserved and transmitted within Judean circles. The accounts of the first two battles attracted no significant changes in the hands of the southerners. But the account of the third, the battle at Ramoth-gilead, received much attention in that it involved a king of Judah (also anonymous following the preceding stage of transmission). This king of Judah was now identified within these Judean circles as Jehosha-

---

24. For a recent traditio-historical analysis of the Elisha cycle, cf. Hans-Christoph Schmitt, *Elisa: traditionsgeschichtliche Untersuchungen zur vorklassischen nordisraelitischen Prophetie* (Güters-loh: Gerd Mohn, 1972). Cf. also Alexander Rofé, "The Classification of the Prophetical Stories," *JBL* 89 (1970), 427–440.

25. The reference to Ahab in 22:20 would have been added after these narratives were incorporated into the Deuteronomistic history. Whether Ben-hadad's name was preserved from the beginning or inserted by the Deutronomistic compilers on the basis of his appearance in the Elisha stories is unclear.

phat, and the narrative revised further to emphasize Jehoshaphat's piety over against that of the king of Israel. The distinctive character of this Judean revision can best be seen by comparing the narrative as it stands now with the account of the Moabite campaign, another northern narrative which was revised similarly. Note the striking parallels in structure and wording:

	And he went and sent word to Jehoshaphat king of Judah, "The king of Moab has rebelled
And he said to Jehoshaphat, "Will you go with me to battle at Ramoth-gilead?" And Jehoshaphat said to the king of Israel, "I am as you are, my people as your people, my horses as your horses."	against me; will you go with me to battle against Moab?" And he said, "I will go; I am as you are, my people as your people, my horses as your horses."
	. . . .
And Jehoshaphat said to the king of Israel, "Inquire first for the word of the LORD."	
. . . .	And Jehoshaphat said, "Is there
. . . "Is there not here another prophet of the LORD of whom we may inquire?" (1 Kings 22:4–5, 7)	no prophet of the LORD here, through whom we may inquire of the LORD?" (2 Kings 3:7, 11)

(4) Finally these narratives were incorporated into the Deuteronomistic history, their placement in Ahab's reign being determined by the references to Jehoshaphat. That is, since the king of Judah who participated in the battle of Ramoth-gilead had been identified now as Jehoshaphat, it naturally followed that the king of Israel involved was Jehoshaphat's contemporary, Ahab. The placement of the Elisha stories was determined similarly. The appearance of Elisha alongside Jehoshaphat and Jehoram in the account of the Moabite campaign implied that Elisha's career began early in Jehoram's reign. Otherwise there is nothing in the traditions preserved in the Deuteronomistic history to suggest that Elisha's career began before the very end of Jehoram's reign (2 Kings 9:1ff.).

The preceding reconstruction of the transmission history of the narrative in 1 Kings 20 and 22:1–38, even if correct only in the broadest limits, obviously has far-reaching implications for the use of these narratives as historical sources. Basically they appear to be authentic reports of actual battles. Yet they have been expanded more than once during the process of transmission and influenced by factors which tend—to say the least—to detract from their historical accuracy. Moreover, the association of these battles with Ahab's reign, as well as the association of the Elisha narratives with Jehoram's reign, appears to have been determined largely by one of these traditio-historical factors—i.e., the identification of the king of Judah who aided the king(s) of Israel at Ramoth-gilead and in the Moabite campaign as Jehoshaphat. It is not at all surprising that those who preserved and transmitted the northern narratives during Judah's late monarchical period would have made this identification. Jehoshaphat was one of Judah's most colorful kings, and he had come to be remembered by tradition as the monarch whose otherwise exemplary reign was marred by an ill-fated alliance with Israel.[26] But was this identification correct?

Actually an increasing number of scholars suspect that these narratives in 1 Kings 20 and 22 also belong in the context of the Jehu dynasty, and that the Ben-hadad who appears in them was Ben-hadad the son of Hazael.[27] This is suggested by the striking similarity of the descriptions of the king of Israel's army at Aphek and Jehoahaz's army (cf. 2 Kings 20:26–27 with 2 Kings 13:7) as well as the references to the cities which Ben-hadad promised to restore as a result of the battle (cf. 1 Kings 20:34 with 2 Kings 13:24–25). The Moabite campaign is probably to be associated with Jehoram's reign. But Jehoshaphat could hardly have been the king of Judah who aided Jehoram. For one thing, as we shall see below, the reigns of Jehoshaphat and Jehoram probably did not overlap.

To summarize: If the historian, as a result of his critical analysis, concludes that the Deuteronomistic compilers erred in their placement of the narratives in 1 Kings 20; 22:1–38 and the Elisha stories; if he concludes, specifically, that these narratives reflect conditions and circumstances of the Jehu rather than the Omride dynasty; then he is left with quite a different picture of the Omride period from the one received from a non-critical reading of 1–2 Kings. There remain only indications that the Omrides, especially Omri and Ahab, ruled over a wealthy and autonomous kingdom (indicated, for example, by their building projects) and that they commanded unusually strong armies in comparison to those of their immediate neighbors (Omri's conquest of Moab; Ahab's two thousand chariots and ten thousand foot soldiers at Qarqar). In addition to their alliances with Phoenicia and Judah

---

26. This alliance would have been all too well remembered, since it led to one of the darkest days of Judah's early history. In fact, the assassination of Ahaziah of Judah (2 Kings 9:27–28) followed by Althaliah's seizure of the Judean throne and execution of the remaining members of the royal family (2 Kings 11:1ff.) constituted the most serious threat to the continuation of the Davidic dynasty throughout Judah's monarchical history. Cf. especially the treatment of Jehoshaphat's reign in 2 Chronicles 17–20.

27. Cf. A. Jepsen, "Israel und Damaskus," AfOF, 14 (1942), 154–158; G. F. Whitley, "The Deuteronomic Presentation of the House of Omri"; E. Lipinski, "Le Ben-Hadad II de la Bible et L'histoire," Proceedings of the Fifth World Congress of Jewish Studies (Jerusalem: R. H. Hacohen Press, 1969), pp. 157–173. This is also my own position, expressed in the articles cited in note 17.

which were sealed by royal marriages (Jezebel and Ahab, Athaliah and Jehoram of Judah), they supported the Aramaean kingdoms of Hamath and Damascus in a successful effort to halt the advance of Assyrian armies on at least one and possibly several occasions.

The evidences of Omride/Aramaean hostilities disappear entirely when the narratives in question are disqualified as authentic sources for the Omride period and associated instead with the period of the Jehu dynasty, except for Hazael's encroachment in the northern Transjordan (Ramoth-gilead) at the very end of Jehoram's reign. The apparent conflicts between these narratives and Shalmaneser's inscriptions are also resolved. The pitiful army described in 1 Kings 20:26–27 belonged not to Ahab but to one of Jehu's successors. The Ben-hadad who appears in 1 Kings 20:1ff. and in the Elisha stories was not Hadadezer by another name, but a later ruler of Damascus, the son of Hazael.

Textual Criticism

The Deuteronomistic history provides for each of the kings of Israel and Judah (1) a synchronistic date which locates the beginning of their reign in relation to that of the contemporary ruler of the other kingdom and (2) a reckoning of their regnal period, i.e., the number of years which they reigned. Ahab's reign is introduced typically:

In the thirty-eighth year of Asa king of Judah, Ahab the son of Omri began to reign over Israel, and Ahab the son of Omri reigned over Israel in Samaria twenty-two years. (1 Kings 16:29)

These synchronisms and regnal reckonings are crucial for reconstructing the chronology of the Divided Kingdoms. Yet they are problematic in a number of ways. The regnal periods do not always correspond to the requirements of the synchronistic dates. Neither can we be certain that the two kingdoms employed the same calendars or systems of reckoning. It would have made a difference in calculating the synchronisms and regnal periods, for example, if one of the kingdoms used a spring-to-spring calendar while the other used an autumn-to-autumn calendar. Whether the kings' accession dates and/or regnal periods were figured from the time they actually began to rule, or whether they were figured from the coronation ceremony, which itself may have occurred in conjunction with the annual new year festival, would have made further differences.[28] Finally, and most problematic of all, the available manuscripts often provide variant readings.

28. On these matters, cf. J. Finegan, *Handbook of Biblical Chronology* (Princeton: Princeton University Press, 1964).

The complications and variant textual readings are especially numerous for the Omride period. It has been observed, in fact, that two different patterns of synchronistic dates are preserved for the period, one which dominates the Masoretic tradition (i.e., the traditional Hebrew manuscripts), and one which dominates the Greek manuscripts of the so-called Lucianic recension.[29] A certain amount of textual interaction has taken place. As they stand now both the Masoretic and the Lucianic manuscripts contain elements of both patterns. But the foreign elements can be deleted with some confidence by close textual analysis, and the two patterns emerge as follows:

Kings of Israel	MT	LXX^L
Ahab	38th year of Asa	2nd year of Jehoshaphat
Ahaziah	17th of Jehoshaphat	24th of Jehoshaphat
Jehoram	18th of Jehoshaphat	2nd of Jehoram
Kings of Judah		
Jehosphaphat	4th of Ahab	11th of Omri
Jehoram	5th of Jehoram	?
Ahaziah	11th of Jehoram	?

The Lucianic synchromisms for the accession of Jehoram and Ahaziah of Judah are missing. But it is clear from the other synchronisms of that pattern that Jehoram of Judah would have ascended the throne during the brief reign of Ahaziah of Israel.

The main difference between the two patterns is that the one dominating the Masoretic tradition dates the kings of Judah later in relation to the kings of Israel, and vice versa. Note further in this regard that the account of the Moabite campaign in 2 Kings 3:4ff.—i.e., as it stands now with the kings of Israel and Judah identified as Jehoram and Jehoshaphat—is not in keeping wtih the Lucianic pattern. According to the Lucianic pattern the reigns of these two kings did not overlap; Jehoram did not ascend the throne until the second year of Jehoshaphat's son. The Masoretic pattern, on the other hand, is probably to be understood as a revision, intended to meet the chronological requirements of the Moabite campaign account by shifting the reigns of the kings of Israel and Judah far enough in relation to each other to allow Jehoram's and Jehoshaphat's reigns to overlap.

If one is prepared to posit various extenuating circumstances which are not indicated in the texts (changes in calendars or systems of reckoning, coregencies, etc.) it is possible to construct from the figures

29. Cf. J. D. Shenkel, *Chronology and Recensional Development in the Greek Text of Kings* (Cambridge: Harvard University Press, 1968); and R. W. Klein, *Textual Criticism of the Old Testament*, Guides to Biblical Scholarship: Old Testament Series (Philadelphia: Fortress Press, 1975), pp. 36–42.

provided by the Masoretic tradition a chronology in which all the pieces fit. A weakness of this approach is that, with unlimited appeal to such extenuating circumstances, almost any set of figures within reason could be made to fit. The more serious problem is that this approach does not allow for the complexities involved in the history of the transmission of the manuscripts. The variant figures provided for Jehoram's reign in 2 Kings 1:17 and 3:1 (second year of Jehoram of Judah/eighteenth year of Jehoshaphat) serve as an example. This conflict can be neatly resolved, as noted above, by positing a coregency between Jehoshaphat and his son beginning in the former's seventeenth year. But careful textual analysis with proper attention to variant readings in the Greek manuscripts has revealed that the synchronism in 2 Kings 1:17 (second year of Jehoram) is a remnant of the Lucianic pattern which otherwise has been expunged from the Hebrew texts. Thus any attempt to harmonize this synchronism with the other Masoretic figures can only produce misleading results. Moreover, if the Masoretic figures represent a revision of an earlier chronology which is preserved more accurately in the Lucianic pattern, as textual analysis also seems to indicate, then any chronological reconstruction of the Omride period which begins with the Masoretic figures is misguided.

POSSIBILITIES OF INTERPRETATION

The situation which the historian encounters in connection with the Omride/Aramaean question is typical in the study of biblical history. The ancient written sources provide only limited and often ambiguous information. Yet they are specific enough that conflicts are recognizable in their testimonies. Moreover, these conflicts arise already in the biblical texts; it is sometimes, but certainly not always, a matter of biblical against non-biblical claims. When ancient historians disagree on matters such as the Omride/Aramaean question, generally it is not because they are depending upon different sources, but because they are assessing and interpreting these same sources differently.

The range of possibilities for interpreting the historical implications of the ancient sources often is quite broad, as was illustrated in the preceding discussion. Two essentially different approaches emerged. One approach is characterized by its confidence in the historical accuracy of the ancient documents, the tendency of this approach being to harmonize their testimonies insofar as possible. Conflicts are handled by positing extenuating circumstances which the documents do not actually specify, but which seem necessary in order to harmonize their testimonies. The hypothesis that "Ben-hadad" was Hadadezer's throne name and the positing of a coregency for Jehoshaphat and his son are explanations of this sort. The other approach is characterized by suspicion of the testimony of the ancient texts. Conflicts in their testimonies are seen as warning signals that misleading historical information is at hand. These conflicts are to be sought out and explained by means of literary criticism, form criticism, etc. The Ben-hadad/Hadadezer conflict is explained in accordance with this approach as the result of misplaced narratives in the Deuteronomistic history, and the conflicting synchronisms for Jehoram in terms of secondary revisions of the manuscripts.

The idea is not that the historian should favor either of these approaches to the exclusion of the other, although that is sometimes the case. Rather, he should constantly explore the possibilities of both as he goes about his research. Sometimes conflicts in the sources are apparent rather than real. They are clues to extenuating circumstances not spelled out in the text; and if the historian can clarify these circumstances he has in effect added to our historical knowledge. On other occasions the sources are simply misleading, and to posit extenuating circumstances which allow for the validity of their testimonies is, to the extent that such hypotheses gain acceptance, to produce fictitious history.

Thus the historian of Old Testament times is constantly engaged in a "lover's quarrel" with the ancient written sources. He is dependent upon them and must listen carefully to their testimonies even when they seem to conflict. Yet he must be ever suspicious of their claims, and never jump to conclusions without thoroughly analyzing them with the best critical tools available. Too many factors have entered into their formulation and transmission from ancient times to the present to overlook this crucial step.

III

Interpreting the Artifactual Evidence

We have already observed that the artifactual remains recovered by archaeologists (surface pottery, fragments of walls, floor levels, etc.) usually provide only the most general sort of historical information (the locations of ancient cities, approximate dates of their occupational phases, some indications of the life styles of their inhabitants, etc.). Occasionally the artifactual remains witness to specific events (a city's destruction by fire, a public building remodeled and expanded, etc.). But these events also remain anonymous unless interpreted in the light of written records. Thus it is rarely a matter of the historian drawing conclusions from artifactual evidence in and of itself but rather of his interpreting the artifactual evidence along with, and in the context of, his written sources. The purpose of this chapter is to illustrate the inter-relationship between artifactual and written evidence in the historian's research. Again our example is especially relevant for the study of the Omride period. That is, we will focus our attention on the archaeological excavations at *Sebaṣṭiyeh*, probably the site of biblical Samaria, the royal residence of the Omride kings.

SEBAṢṬÎYEH: AN ARCHAEOLOGICAL SITE EXAMINED

The ruins of *Sebaṣṭiyeh* are located in the northern part of the central Palestinian hill country, on a hill approximately three hundred feet above the surrounding valley. The ancient city to which the ruins belong, besides having been located in a rich and fertile area, would have commanded lines of communication east-west across the hill country and northward via Dothan to the plains of Jezreel. Scholars were already confident that this ancient city was biblical Samaria before archaeological excavations were undertaken at the site: (1) The Arab name *Sebaṣṭiyeh* and surface Roman ruins strongly suggested that this was the site of the Roman Sebastie built by Herod. (2)

Classical writers, particularly Eusebius,[1] equated Herod's Sebastie with biblical Samaria. (3) If we consider especially the communications connections, the site of Sebasṭîyeh would have been ideal for the Omride residence and the capital of the northern kingdom.

Thus, when a team of archaeologists sponsored by Harvard University undertook to excavate Sebasṭîyeh in 1908–1910,[2] they already had some idea as to what they would find. In regard to the Israelite phase of the city's history, for example, they knew from 1 Kings 16:24 that Omri had founded the city on an essentially virgin site, from 1 Kings 16:32 and 22:39 that a second building phase had occurred during Ahab's reign, and from 2 Kings 17 that the city was conquered by Assyria during the latter part of the eighth century (i.e., approximately a century and a half after its founding). The results of their excavations corresponded closely enough to expectations to consider the Sebasṭîyeh/Sebastie/Samaria equation confirmed. The debris which rested on virgin rock did indeed produce objects which could be associated confidently with the period of the Divided Kingdoms (including the Samaria Ostraca mentioned in Chapter I, p. 10). Moreover, the massiveness and construction technique of the buildings and walls which occupied the hill during the Israelite period were strongly suggestive of a royal quarter. The excavators identified three building phases for these Israelite structures which they assigned respectively to Omri, Ahab, and Jeroboam II.

Excavations were undertaken at Sebasṭîyeh again in 1931–35, sponsored jointly this time by the Palestine Exploration Fund, the British Academy, the British School of Archaeology in Jerusalem, the Hebrew University in Jerusalem, and Harvard University.[3] Miss Kathleen Kenyon of the British School was in charge of excavating a strip across the summit of the hill. With careful attention to the stratigraphy of the ruins and typological analysis of the pottery she distinguished five occupational phases for the Israelite period.

Phases I-II (the Omride city). Construction of phase I would have begun in 880 B.C. according to the chronology followed by Kenyon— i.e., the date of Omri's transferral of the royal residence from Tirza to Samaria. Phase II is to be attributed primarily or entirely to Ahab. This

1. Eusebius, *Das Onomastikon der biblischen Ortsnamen*, ed. E. Klostermann (Hildesheim: Georg Olms Verlagsbuchhandlung, 1966), pp. 154–155, lines 21–25.
2. G. A. Reisner, C. S. Fisher, and D. G. Lyon, *Harvard Excavations at Samaria, 1908–1910* (Cambridge: Harvard University Press, 1924), 2 vols.
3. J. W. Crowfoot, K. M. Kenyon, E. L. Sukenik, *Samaria-Sebaste I: The Buildings* (London: Palestine Exploration Fund, 1942); J. W. Crowfoot and G. M. Crowfoot, *Samaria-Sebaste II: Early Ivories* (London: Palestine Exploration Fund, 1938); J. W. Crowfoot, G. M. Crowfoot, K. M. Kenyon, *Samaria-Sebaste III: The Objects* (London: Palestine Exploration Fund, 1957).

latter is the most impressive of the five Israelite phases with regard to massiveness and construction technique, and reflects close similarities to Phoenician architecture. Phases I-II were not distinguishable from each other on ceramic grounds. Their pottery, taken together, was described by the excavators as typical of the tenth and ninth centuries B.C. Remnants of ivory inlays found mainly in the debris which covered the remains of the buildings of phases IV-V were also assigned primarily to Ahab's reign.

Phase III (Jehu's city). This phase of the city's occupation was distinguished from the one preceding on the basis of: (1) the appearance of structures on the summit of the hill which were of poorer building technique than those of phase II and which tended to disregard the latter's plan; (2) a similar occurrence in connection with a phase I enclosure wall (number 161 in the excavation reports) on the middle terrace which had remained in use through phase II; and (3) a slight but noticeable typological development in the pottery. Since the phase III structures tended to disregard the plan of phase II, yet were of poorer building technique, it was concluded that the phase II structures must have been destroyed under circumstances other than for the purpose of rebuilding. Specifically, the excavators attributed their destruction to the political and military disturbances which supposedly rocked the northern kingdom during the last years of the Omride period. According to the 1-2 Kings account, as we saw in Chapter II, these disturbances were set into motion by Ahab's death at Ramoth-gilead and led finally to Jehu's massacre of the Omride family and seizure of the throne in Samaria (i.e., during the 850's B.C.). The transition between phases III and IV-V, on the other hand, was attributed to disruptions created by the Aramaean wars which reached a climax during Jehoahaz's reign (i.e., ca. 800 B.C.).

Phases IV-V (between the Aramaean wars and the Assyrian conquest; ca. 800-722 B.C.). These two phases were also indicated by noticeable changes in building plan on the summit of the site and further gradual typological development in the pottery. Ceramic differences were observable between phases III and IV, but not between IV and V. Taken together, the pottery and other objects (e.g., seal impressions) of phases IV-V call for a date sometime in the eighth century B.C.[4]

4. The ostraca, which the original excavators assigned to Ahab's building phase, had in the meantime been reassigned to the second quarter of the eighth century on the basis of ceramic and paleographical considerations. This would place them contemporary with phases IV-V. A wall and associated fill pottery on the middle terrace must be placed at the very end of phase V. It was unclear to the excavators whether this wall was built just before or just after Sargon's conquest of the city. In the latter case it would properly be referred to as phase VI.

ARTIFACTUAL EVIDENCE, WRITTEN EVIDENCE

The interpretation of the *Sebasṭiyeh* materials summarized above has gained almost unanimous acceptance by scholars, with minor modifications here and there, and the results cited again and again as an example of how archaeological evidence has confirmed and expanded upon the biblical record. The following statement from John Bright's *A History of Israel* is typical.

Archaeology has shown [italics mine] that the city begun by Omri and completed by Ahab had fortifications unequalled in ancient Palestine for excellence of workmanship. Ivory inlays found in one of the buildings (the earliest of the Samaria ivories come from that period) may illustrate the "ivory house" that Ahab is said to have built. . . .[5]

My intention here is not to challenge this commonly accepted interpretation of the *Sebasṭiyeh* materials, but to point out that this interpretation depends much more upon written sources already available before the excavations began at *Sebasṭiyeh* than upon the artifactual data uncovered there. What we learn from the artifactual remains themselves is that a city stood at *Sebasṭiyeh* during the Iron Age, that it was conceivably of royal status, that it witnessed five building and occupational phases beginning sometime in the tenth/ninth century B.C. and ending sometime in the eighth century, and that its inhabitants participated in the common Syro-Palestinian culture of the day (Phoenician building techniques, carved ivory inlays, ostraca written in a Canaanite dialect, etc.). It is on the basis of written records, primarily Eusebius and the Bible, that this city is identified as Samaria, the capital of the northern kingdom, and the occupational phases are assigned to Omri, Ahab, Jehu, etc. Moreover, when the artifactual data seems out of keeping with the biblical record, it is clearly the latter which takes precedence in the interpretation summarized above. Two examples may be cited, the first having to do with the pottery associated with phases I-II and the second with the stratigraphy of the ivories.

The excavators described the earliest Iron Age pottery from the site,[6] that associated with building phase I, as typical of the tenth and ninth centuries B.C. Actually, especially in the light of more recent excavations at other Iron Age sites, this pottery seems more typical of the tenth century than of the ninth. It finds it closest parallels, for example, in the Solomonic stratum of Hazor (Stratum X). Much energy has been expended, therefore, in attempts to explain why Omri's city would have begun with, and apparently continued to produce for some

5. John Bright, *A History of Israel* (Philadelphia: Westminster Press, 1972²), p. 240.
6. A small amount of Early Bronze Age pottery was also discovered at the site.

time, pottery characteristic of the preceding century! The discrepancy can be eased somewhat, but not resolved, by presuming that Omri's builders brought pottery of earlier manufacture with them when they began to work at the site. Another proposal is that there was actually a tenth-century, pre-Omride settlement at *Sebastiyeh* which Omri's builders razed to the ground.[7] But this proposal is counter to the implications of 1 Kings 16:24 that Omri purchased an unoccupied hill for his new capital, and undercuts the grounds for assigning phase I to Omri at all. Kenyon insists that the apparent ceramic discrepancy is due to misleading recording procedures employed by the excavators of Hazor and certain other sites:

In the Samaria excavations, the British method was followed, by which the pottery and other finds ascribed to a structural period are those actually associated with the building operation, from the foundation trenches, floor make-up, and so on. Admittedly such fills will include earlier, derived material, together with that dropped by the builders, but it is a commonplace of British archaeology that a building is dated by the last object in its building deposits. The method at Hazor and most other Near Eastern sites is different. The material assigned to a stratum is that above its floors. There are two objections to this. In the absence of any published sections observed and drawn in the field (as distinct from schematic ones built up from a collection of theodolite levels) at Hazor, there is no means of telling whether the objects come from one or more successive occupation levels, from destruction debris or from subsequent robber disturbance. There is no evidence as to how the objects from its construction levels are ascribed; presumably they are just incorporated in the material belonging to the lower stratum. Secondly, it has been emphasized by many excavators that the majority of the finds on the floor of a building represent its final use. Professor Albright's excavations at Tell Beit Mirsim provide an excellent sample. Stratum B3 was destroyed ca. 930 B.C. It was immediately succeeded by Stratum A, which was destroyed in 588 B.C. Almost all the pottery is late seventh–early sixth century. Therefore if Stratum A is dated by its latest pottery, it is sixth century B.C. In exactly the same way Hazor Stratum X is not dated by the pottery published as Stratum X, but this provides an indication for the time Stratum X continued in use and a *terminus post quem* for the building of Stratum IX. There is no great harm in this, provided it is understood how the evidence is to be interpreted. But the converse is extremely important. Hazor Stratum X is Solomonic, but the pottery from Stratum X is *not* Solomonic, or at least not necessarily so; its date depends on the date of the construction of IX.[8]

But rather than restoring confidence in the date assigned to phase I, Kathleen Kenyon's explanation emphasizes and illustrates the lack of

7. Cf. Yohanan Aharoni and Ruth Amiran, "A New Scheme for the Sub-Division of the Iron Age in Palestine," *IEJ* 8 (1958), 171–184, esp. 179–180.
8. K. M. Kenyon, "Megiddo, Hazor, Samaria and Chronology," *University of London Institute of Archaeology Bulletin* 4 (1964), 145–146.

standardization in contemporary archaeological methodology and the highly subjective nature of archaeological dating procedures in general. In spite of her explanation one must suspect that, if the statement in 1 Kings 16:24 had been unavailable and phase I had been dated purely on the basis of the artifactual evidence, it would have been assigned without hesitation to the tenth century.

The Phoenician architecture which characterizes the buildings of phase II appears in Israelite cities as early as the tenth century (Megiddo) and as late as the sixth century (Ramat-Rahel). There is nothing about this building style itself, in other words, any more than about the corresponding pottery, which will enable the archaeologist to date phase II to Ahab's reign.[9] The evidence for connecting this phase with Ahab is 1 Kings 16:31–32, which indicates that Ahab married a Phoenician wife and undertook building projects in Samaria with her interests in mind. Likewise, the reference in 1 Kings 22:39 to the "house of ivory" which Ahab built, presumably in Samaria, is the key evidence for assigning the numerous ivory fragments discovered in the debris at Sebastiyeh to Ahab. Other arguments can be marshaled in support of an Ahab date for the ivories once they have already been assigned on the basis of the biblical record: a few scattered fragments were found in the earlier strata of the debris; the ivories reflect similarities to others found in Assyria (Nimrud, Arslan Tash) which would also allow a ninth-century date; they are the sort of item which would have remained in use over a long period of time. But the fact remains that the bulk of these ivory fragments were found in the debris which covered the ruins of phases IV-V, and one must again suspect that if they were assigned on the basis of purely archaeological procedures, rather than under the influence of 1 Kings 22:39, they would have been associated primarily with phases IV-V.

Thus the statement quoted above from John Bright's history of Israel is somewhat misleading. Archaeology itself has neither shown the character of workmanship of the city begun by Omri nor illustrated Ahab's ivory house. What it has done is recover the remains of an ancient city which was already generally agreed to be Samaria before excavations began; and, not without some effort, these remains have been interpreted and dated in accordance with information derived from the Bible about Samaria's history. The artifacts themselves told

---

9. It is true that a vessel bearing the name of Osorkon II, a contemporary of Ahab, was found in one of the buildings on the citadel. But this could hardly have played a decisive role in dating phase II, since the vessel was found in context with the ostraca, which in turn were attributed by the excavators to Jeroboam II.

us nothing about Omri or Ahab until they were interpreted in the context of the written evidence.

This distinction between what can be learned from the artifacts alone and what is to be learned when they are interpreted in connection with written sources becomes especially crucial when the written sources involved are themselves open to divergent interpretations. Let us consider one more example from *Sebasṭiyeh*. The excavators associated the transition between phases II and III with the political and military disturbances which supposedly rocked Samaria following Ahab's death at Ramoth-gilead (1 Kings 22:1–38) and led to Jehu's seizure of the throne (2 Kings 9:1–10:27). Accordingly, the end of phase II is dated in the 850's B.C., and the beginning of phase III in the 840's. The ceramic evidence is simply not precise enough to establish so close a dating. Neither do the remains of the phase II buildings necessarily call for the conclusion that their abandonment and replacement were associated with political and/or military disturbances. There are various other possible explanations—e.g., the buildings may have been irreparably damaged by an earthquake. Here again, therefore, it becomes apparent that dates for the archaeological phases at Samaria have been established, not on the basis of artifactual evidence as such, but on the basis of a rather arbitrary and unverifiable combination of artifactual evidence with the testimony of 1–2 Kings. More to the point, we have already seen in the preceding chapter that precisely those narratives in 1–2 Kings which associate Ahab with a battle at Ramoth-gilead (1 Kings 20; 22:1–38) and imply that his death there was followed by a period of civil and international strife for the northern kingdom (2 Kings 6:8–23; 6:24–7:20) may well be out of place in the Deuteronomistic history. If so, the grounds upon which the end of phase II and the beginning of phase III have been dated disappear altogether. There is no longer reason to suppose that Samaria suffered violence during the 850's or 840's B.C. Hazael's attack at the end of Jehoram's reign was upon Ramoth-gilead in the northern Transjordan, not Samaria (2 Kings 8:29ff.). Jehu's *coup d'état* was a violent moment for Samaria. But the unusually full account we have of this incident clearly implies that the property damage was limited to a Baalistic temple (2 Kings 9:1–10:27, cf. especially vss. 10:24–28).

THE HISTORIAN'S USE OF ARCHAEOLOGICAL DATA

The artifactual evidence recovered by archaeologists is an extremely important source of information for the historian of ancient times. The purpose of the preceding comments is not to belittle the usefulness of such data for the biblical historian—any more than it is to issue a call for a full-scale reinterpretation of the *Sebasṭiyeh* materials—but to emphasize the caution with which the historian must proceed as he seeks to utilize archaeological evidence in his reconstruction of the past events. Warning is in order at three points:

(1) Archaeological methodology is constantly developing in precision and sophistication. It goes without saying that conclusions reached by earlier generations of excavators must be checked again and again in the light of more recent developments and discoveries. But archaeological research as it is practiced today still involves a great deal of subjective and intuitive judgment. Moreover, as Kenyon's statement quoted above clearly indicates, archaeological procedures are still by no means standardized. Therefore archaeological excavation reports must never be read with attention only to the conclusions reached by the excavators. The historian, if he is to assess the validity of these conclusions properly, must be attentive as well to the excavation and recording methodologies employed, and especially cautious when the conclusions are influenced by non-artifactual considerations.[10]

(2) Obviously, when a written source has served as a determining factor in the interpretation of any given archaeological data, it is misleading to cite the interpreted archaeological data in turn as "proof" of the accuracy of the written source. If at all, it is legitimate to speak in terms of archaeological proof only when there is a significant amount of controlled archaeological data available, when all of this data has been taken into account, and when it is not susceptible to alternative interpretations. The circular argumentation which can occur reaches its extremes in certain books which seek to demonstrate that archaeological findings prove the historical accuracy of the Bible as read uncritically.[11] The most these books demonstrate is that if one is already predisposed toward a non-critical approach to the Bible, a certain amount of archaeological data can be interpreted in accordance with such an approach. The data which do not fit so well into such a scheme generally go unmentioned.

(3) When written and artifactual evidence exist side-by-side, the artifacts generally depend heavily upon the written sources for their interpretation. Yet we have seen that the written sources themselves are often open to divergent interpretations and can be misleading. This

10. Cf. H. J. Franken and C. A. Franken-Battershill, *A Primer of Old Testament Archaeology* (Leiden: E. J. Brill, 1963), esp. pp. 19–33.
11. An especially notorious book of this genre is Werner Keller's *The Bible as History* (New York: William Morrow, 1956). It is a translation of a German original entitled *Und die Bibel hat doch recht* (The Bible Was Right After All).

means that the critical historian must maintain a distinction, at least in his own mind, between the conclusions which can be reached from the artifacts in and of themselves, and the conclusions he reaches in the process of interpreting these artifacts in the light of the written evidence. Otherwise he may lapse into the same sort of circular argumentation mentioned above. This would occur if he advanced a hypothesis regarding some historical circumstance or event based on his analysis of the written sources, proceeded to demonstrate that the available artifactual data could be made to fit the hypothesis, and then, since it could be made to fit, presumed that archaeology supported the hypothesis. It is legitimate to claim that archaeology supports a position only when enough distinctive archaeological evidence is available for judgment and when the possible alternative interpretations of the same evidence have been taken into account.

IV

Israel's Early History: Three Debated Issues

The Old Testament provides us with a number of very useful sources for reconstructing Israel's history during the monarchical period and following, some of which originated roughly contemporary with the circumstances and events which they describe. For example, the so-called Throne Succession Narrative (2 Sam. 9–20; 1 Kings 1–2) appears to be a first-hand account of David's last years on the throne and of the transferral of the crown to Solomon.[1] Some of the data recorded in 1–2 Kings regarding the reigns of Solomon and the subsequent rulers of the Divided Kingdoms probably derives ultimately from official court records. The non-biblical documents of the ancient Near East, especially the royal inscriptions of Israel's neighbors, also provide a significant amount of direct information for Israelite history beginning in the ninth century B.C. (i.e., the Omride period and following). This relative abundance of roughly contemporary documentary evidence does not mean, of course, that the task of reconstructing Israel's monarchical and post-monarchical history is easy. Even eyewitness accounts, when we have them, can be biased or misleading and must always be evaluated critically. The preceding two chapters illustrate the sorts of historical issues and problems which can arise even for a period as well documented as that of the Omride dynasty.

Nevertheless, the difficulties increase when the historian turns his attention to Israel's early history, prior to the establishment of the monarchy, for which the sources are scarce and far more problematic. Even the question of when to begin to speak of Israel as an historical entity is an open one, and emerges from the biblical texts themselves. Note that, while the Genesis account gives full attention to the "sojournings" of Abraham and somewhat less attention to Isaac, it is actually Jacob who bears the name "Israel" in this account and who is

1. Cf. above, Chapter I, note 30.

identified as the immediate common ancestor of the twelve Israelite tribes. Perhaps even in Old Testament times the stories about Abraham and Isaac were perceived as accounts of Israel's "prehistory." For the most part, the biblical sources of information for Israel's origins and pre-monarchical history are folk materials—i.e., folk narratives, genealogies, songs, and the like. The non-biblical documents on the other hand, although they provide valuable information about general circumstances in Syria-Palestine, tell us nothing specific about the Israelite tribes. Admittedly, the list of "minor judges" recorded in Judg. 10:1–5; 12:7–15 may preserve official recollections of some sort.[2] And, as we noted in Chapter I, an Egyptian victory stele dated approximately 1230 B.C. refers to "Israel." But the historical implications of neither of these sources are very clear.

Therefore, in view of this lack of direct information, it is not surprising that historians of Old Testament times diverge much more widely in their views regarding Israel's origins and early history than they do regarding the monarchical period and later. In this chapter we shall review three of the currently debated questions regarding Israel's early history: Was there a "Patriarchal Period"? Did the Hebrew tribes take possession of the land of Canaan by means of a sudden conquest or by gradual settlement? Were these tribes organized in an "amphictyonic" confederacy during the period of the Judges?

WAS THERE A "PATRIARCHAL AGE"?

The biblical account of the sojournings of Abraham, Isaac, and Jacob appears in Genesis 12 and following chapters. The literary character of these chapters need only be summarized here, since it has been discussed in earlier volumes of this series.[3] The account is composite, consisting basically of two strands of material, the so-called Yahwistic and Priestly sources. Most of the narratives in these chapters are Yahwistic. As in the case of the Elisha legends discussed above, they also reflect a lively folk imagination, and emerged orally as independent stories before they were combined into narrative cycles and finally incorporated into the longer written documents. Unlike the

---

2. Cf. esp. Martin Noth, "Das Amt des 'Richters Israels,' " *Festschrift für Alfred Bertholet* (Tübingen: J. C. B. Mohr, 1950), pp. 404–417, reprinted in *Gesammelte Studien zum Alten Testament*, II (München: Chr. Kaiser Verlag, 1969), pp. 71–85; but also W. Richter, "Zu den 'Richtern Israels,' " *ZAW* 77 (1965), 40–72.

3. N. Habel (*Literary Criticism of the Old Testament* [Philadelphia: Fortress Press, 1971]) treats the Yahwistic and Priestly sources. G. M. Tucker (*Form Criticism of the Old Testament* [Philadelphia: Fortress Press, 1971], esp. pp. 29–41) discusses the character of saga in relation to other literary genres. W. E. Rast (*Tradition History and the Old Testament* [Philadelphia: Fortress Press, 1972], esp. pp. 33–56) outlines the process by which the individual sagas were united into narrative cycles and finally incorporated into the longer written documents.

prophetical legends which seek to glorify the prophets by recounting their miraculous deeds, the patriarchal narratives deal with family matters and reflect themes relevant to the self-understanding of the people of Israel as a whole.

In keeping with their focus on personal and family matters, these narratives include no references which allow us to associate the patriarchs with historical persons or events known otherwise.[4] On the contrary, they exhibit characteristics which detract from their usefulness to the historian. It is apparent, for example, that these narratives have been influenced thematically by the names of the characters involved.[5] They abound with folk aetiologies. Israel's possession of the land and her destiny as a great nation are constant themes in them. Also, there is a noticeable concern to legitimize Israelite worship at the originally Canaanite shrines of Shechem, Bethel, Hebron, etc. by indicating that the patriarchs also worshiped at these places (Gen. 12:6, 8; 13:18, etc.). In short, it is apparent that these narratives, at least in their present form, derive from and tell us more about the interests and concerns of an Israel already in possession of the "promised land" than about the history of Israel's origin.

Some historians prefer to leave it at that. According to Julius Wellhausen, for example, writing almost a century ago, "we attain to no historical knowledge of the patriarchs, but only of the time when the stories about them arose in the Israelite people; this later age is here unconsciously projected, in its inner and its outward features, into hoar antiquity, and is reflected there like a glorified mirage."[6] Martin Noth began his widely acclaimed history of Israel with a discussion of the period of the Judges, and treated the patriarchal narratives as "traditions of the sacral confederation" of tribes which he believed existed at that time.[7]

---

4. Genesis 14 mentions four kings whose names have an authentic ring: Amraphel, king of Shinar; Arioch, king of Ellasar; Chedolaomer, king of Elam; and Tidal, king of Goiim. But none of these kings can be identified or dated, and several factors suggest that the story of their campaign into Palestine is fanciful. Cf. esp. J. A. Emerton, "Some False Clues in the Study of Genesis XIV," and "The Riddle of Genesis XIV," VT 21 (1971), 24–47, 403–439.

5. Thus Isaac's name corresponds closely to the verb ṣaḥaq, which means to "laugh," "play," "mock," or "fondle"; and the stories about him are full of word-plays based on this verb. Abraham and Sarah "laughed" in disbelief when told that they would bear a son in their old age (Gen. 17:17; 18:12). Sarah expressed concern that those who heard about it would make "laughter" and "mock" her (21:6). Later she pressed Abraham to send away Hagar and Ishmael when she saw Ishmael "playing" with Isaac (21:9). Isaac "fondled" Rebecca during their sojourn with Abimelech the Philistine and disclosed thereby that she was his wife rather than his sister (26:8).

6. Julius Wellhausen, *Prolegomena to the History of Ancient Israel* (New York: Meridian Library edition, 1957), pp. 318–319. The German original of this work was published first in 1878 and translated into English in 1885.

7. Martin Noth, *The History of Israel*, trans. P. R. Ackroyd (New York: Harper & Row, 1960²), pp. 121–127. We shall speak further below about this confederation of tribes.

Others are convinced, however, that, while the patriarchal narratives may not be historical sources as such, they nevertheless hark back to actual persons (and/or to tribal movements represented as persons in the narratives) who preceded Israel's emergence as a nation and who can be located in history with some precision. W. F. Albright, one of the leading proponents of this latter view over the past thirty years, writes:

As a whole the picture of Genesis is historical, and there is no reason to doubt the general accuracy of the biographical details and the sketches of personality which make the Patriarchs come alive with a vividness unknown to a single extrabiblical character in the whole vast literature of the ancient Near East.[8]

Among those who seek to locate the patriarchs in history, the majority agree with Albright that they belong to the first part of the second millennium B.C. (i.e., roughly 2000–1800 B.C.). This period has come to be popularly referred to, in fact, as the "Patriarchal Age." Another proposal is that they belong to the Late Bronze Age (i.e., roughly 1500–1200 B.C.). Let us review briefly the arguments for both positions.

Early Second Millennium: (1) Ex. 12:40 indicates that the Israelite stay in Egypt lasted 430 years, and 1 Kings 6:1 reckons 480 years from the Exodus to Solomon's building of the temple. The Septuagint reads "440 years" in the latter case, and other biblical passages provide further slightly divergent data. In short, depending upon the combination of passages and readings one uses, it can be said that biblical figures place the entrance into Egypt, and correspondingly the *terminus ad quem* of the "Patriarchal Age," approximately 800–1000 years before the founding of the temple—i.e., somewhere in the vicinity of 2000–1800 B.C.[9] (2) The names of the patriarchs are of a sort which appear already in the second millennium B.C., especially in the eighteenth-century documents recovered from the ruins of ancient Mari (present-day Tell Harîri, situated on the right bank of the Euphrates, not far from Abu Kemal, Syria). (3) Incidents related in the patriarchal narratives are suggestive of customs also reflected in the Mesopotamian documents of the second millenium B.C. The fifteenth-century-B.C. texts

---

8. W. F. Albright *The Biblical Period from Abraham to Ezra* (New York: Harper & Row, 1963), p. 5. For fuller statements of Albright's views regarding the patriarchs, which reflect changes in his thinking during his career, cf. his *From the Stone Age to Christianity* (Baltimore: Johns Hopkins Press, 1940) and "Abram the Hebrew, a New Archaeological Interpretation," *BASOR* 163 (1961), 36–54.

9. Gen. 15:13 presumes a 400-year stay in Egypt; Gal. 3:17 calls for 430 years between Abraham and Moses; the data in Joshua–1 Samuel require more than 500 years from Joshua and the elders to Saul. Bishop Ussher dated the founding of Solomon's temple 1021 B.C., but most contemporary scholars would date it in the 960's B.C.

from Nuzi (present-day Yorghan Tepe in Iraq), which was situated in the hill-country of ancient Assyria, have received much attention in this regard. The following is one of several examples cited by John Bright:

> Again, as Sarah gave her slave Hagar to Abraham as a concubine (ch. 16:1–4), so at Nuzi a marriage contract obliged the wife, if childless, to provide her husband with a substitute. Should a son be born of such a union, the expulsion of the slave wife and her child was forbidden—which explains Abraham's reluctance to send Hagar and Ishmael away (ch. 21:10f.).[10]

(4) Certain passages in the Mesopotamian and Egyptian documents from the early second millennium B.C. have been interpreted as indicative of an Amorite movement, spilling over from Mesopotamia into Syria-Palestine and Egypt. Moreover, artifactual data from roughly the same period in Palestine have been interpreted as evidence of a semi-nomadic invasion and associated by some with the Amorite movements.[11] The patriarchal stories would fit well into such a milieu.

Late Bronze Age: The arguments presented above for dating the patriarchs in the early second millennium are not so convincing or even so relevant as they might seem, and each can be countered with arguments which suggest a Late Bronze Age date for the patriarchs, if we presume of course that they can be dated at all. (1) The chronological data supplied by the biblical texts for pre-monarchical times are internally conflicting, complicated by textual variations, highly schematic,[12] and must be adjusted in any case in connection with the Exodus. Most contemporary scholars, including those who favor an early second millennium date for the patriarchs, agree that the conquest and/or settlement of Canaan must have occurred at the very end of the Late Bronze Age. Specifically, the Exodus is generally placed in the thirteenth century B.C. That being the case it seems reasonable to place the patriarchs not a great deal earlier—i.e., certainly not before the beginning of the Late Bronze Age. This would accord with biblical references which presuppose four generations for the stay in Egypt (Gen. 15:16), count seven generations from Abraham to Moses (Num. 26:57–59), and ten generations from Judah to David (Ruth 4:18–22).

(2) The documentary evidence for Amorite movements is subject to

---

10. John Bright, *A History of Israel* (Philadelphia: Westminster Press, 1972²), p. 71.

11. Cf. esp. G. Posener, J. Bottéro, and K. M. Kenyon, "Syria and Palestine c. 2160–1780 B.C.," *The Cambridge Ancient History*, rev. ed., fasc. 29 (Cambridge: University Press, 1965).

12. We shall speak further in Chapter V about the character of the chronological data supplied by the Old Testament for early Israel.

more than one interpretation. Even more problematic is the artifactual evidence for a semi-nomadic invasion of Syria-Palestine at approximately the same time. The procedure by which these two different kinds of evidence have been combined with each other and with the biblical materials to produce the "Amorite hypothesis" borders on circular argumentation.[13] But the major problem in the attempt to associate Israel's patriarchs with the Amorites of the early second millennium B.C. is the fact that the biblical records specifically associate them instead with the Aramaeans. The latter began to appear on the fringes of the Syro-Arabian desert near the end of the Late Bronze Age and established kingdoms which were to flourish contemporary with Israel and Judah during the Iron Age. One should perhaps not make too much of Gen. 11:31, which identifies Ur of the Chaldeans (an Aramaean people) as Abraham's home, since this verse is textually problematic and the tradition plays no significant role in the patriarchal narratives. On the other hand these narratives, as well as the biblical genealogies, presuppose throughout close kinship ties between Israel and Nahor's descendants who are clearly identified as Aramaeans (cf. esp. Gen. 25:20; 31:20). The most explicit biblical reference regarding Israel's Aramaean connections, of course, is the creedal statement in Deut. 26:5ff. which begins, "A wandering Aramean was my father; and he went down into Egypt and sojourned there. . . ."

(3) It is exciting to find names similar to those of the patriarchs in the non-biblical documents of the ancient Near East. Nothing can be concluded from this regarding the historicity or date of the patriarchs, however, since it becomes increasingly apparent from the study of these documents that their names were of a fairly common sort and by no means peculiar to the early second millennium. The same applies to the customs reflected in the patriarchal narratives. Studies in the extra-biblical documents of the ancient Near East have shed much new light on these customs, but have provided no evidence for dating them to any specific period. The Genesis-Nuzi parallels in particular have been greatly exaggerated.[14] Moreover, the Nuzi texts themselves date not from the early second millenium, but from the early part of the Late Bronze Age (ca. 1500–1400 B.C.).

---

13. Cf. esp. the devastating analyses of this line of argument by T. L. Thompson, *The Historicity of the Patriarchal Narratives, BZAW* 133 (Berlin: Walter de Gruyter, 1974), pp. 67–171.

14. Cf., e.g., M. Greenberg, "Another Look at Rachel's Theft of the Teraphim," *JBL* 81 (1962), 239–248; J. van Seters, "The Problem of Childlessness in Near Eastern Law and the Patriarchs of Israel," *JBL* 87 (1968), 401–408; "Jacob's Marriages and Ancient Near Eastern Customs: A Re-examination," *HTR* 62 (1968), 377–395; H. Donner, "Adoption oder Legitimation? Erwägungen zur Adoption im Alten Testament auf dem Hintergrund der altorientalischen Rechte," *OA* 8 (1969), 87–119.

Actually, the most explicit dating clues to be found in the patriarchal materials point to neither the early second millennium nor to the Late Bronze Age, but to the Iron Age—i.e., the period of the Judges and following. For example, the references to the Philistines (Gen. 21:34; 26:6–22) can hardly be dated earlier than the twelfth century B.C.; and of course there are still the references to the Chaldeans (Gen. 11:31; 15:7), who probably did not settle in southern Mesopotamia before the beginning of the tenth century. Such references are generally disregarded as anachronisms by those who date the patriarchs during the Bronze Age. The Aramaean references must be disposed of in the same fashion if the patriarchs are to be associated with the Amorites of the early second millennium. But this raises the methodological issue regarding the criteria to be used in deciding which elements in the patriarchal narratives are anachronistic and which are not. In fact, it brings us back full circle to the question of whether there was a patriarchal age at all—i.e., whether Wellhausen was correct in insisting that the patriarchal stories are anachronistic to the core.

SUDDEN CONQUEST OR GRADUAL SETTLEMENT?

The Deuteronomistic history depicts the taking of Canaan as a sudden military conquest by a unified Israel under the leadership of Joshua (Joshua 1–12). The completeness of this conquest, according to the Deuteronomistic perspective, is indicated by the following summary remarks which conclude the account:

Thus the LORD gave to Israel all the land which he swore to give to their fathers; and having taken possession of it, they settled there. And the LORD gave them rest on every side just as he had sworn to their fathers; not one of all their enemies had withstood them, for the LORD had given all their enemies into their hands. (Josh. 21:43–44)

It is readily conceded by virtually all biblical scholars, however, that the Deuteronomistic compilers have presented us with an oversimplified and ideal picture of how Israel came to possess the land. The divergence of opinion on the matter has to do rather with the *extent* to which the Deuteronomistic view is historically unrealistic.

Clues that the Israelite taking of the land occurred more gradually and was due to a less than unified tribal effort emerge from a close examination of the pre-Deuteronomistic narratives and lists which the compilers and editors incorporated into Joshua-Judges. In the first place, the narratives in Joshua 1–11 do not begin to account for the conquest of the whole land. Those in the first ten chapters focus almost entirely on the small tribal territory of Benjamin. Josh. 10:16–42 describes a military campaign into the southern hill country, and Josh. 11:1–15 records a northern campaign into the vicinity of Hazor. But both of these campaigns—even if one disregards the literary-critical and traditio-historical problems involved[15]—appear also to have been relatively localized affairs. The description of the division of the territory among the tribes (Joshua 13–22) begins with a reference to "much land" which apparently had been conquered only in theory and thus remained "to be possessed" (13:1b–6). Judges 1 seems to imply that the taking of the land occurred as the result of individual tribal probes, and includes a long list of cities, some of the most important ones in the land, whose inhabitants the various tribes were unable to drive out (cf. also Josh. 17:14–18).

The conquest narratives in Joshua 1–11, like the prophetical narratives in 1 and 2 Kings and the patriarchal narratives in Genesis, exhibit evidences of a long and complicated transmission history.[16] We can safely assume that some of them hark back to actual historical events. For example, the account in Joshua of the establishment of the covenant with the Gibeonites probably preserves the memory of an early agreement of some sort which was broken later by Saul (cf. 2 Sam. 21:1–14). But other of these narratives may be entirely aetiological or cultic in origin; and even those which are based on actual historical events have undergone such extensive changes during the process of transmission that their historical significance can rarely be determined with any degree of confidence.

The account of the conquest of 'Ai (chs. 7–8) is a case in point. The preceding account of the conquest of Jericho emphasizes that victory over the inhabitants of the land was to be given by Yahweh and was in no way dependent upon human might. Israel's responsibility was to remain faithful and to follow the regulations prescribed for this "holy war."[17] The opening of the 'Ai account continues the holy war theme— i.e., Israel's initial defeat (7:2ff.) illustrates her helplessness in warfare when the prescribed regulations were not maintained in every detail. The description of the tactics which Joshua employed in the second,

---

15. Cf. esp. V. Fritz, "Die sogenannte Liste der besiegten Könige in Josua 12," *ZDPV* 85 (1969), 136–161; and "Das Ende der spätbronzezeitlichen Stadt Hazor Stratum XIII und die biblische Überlieferung in Josua 11 und Richter 4," *UF* 5 (1973), 123–139.

16. Cf. J. A. Soggin, *Joshua*, trans. R. A. Wilson (Philadelphia: Westminster Press, 1972), pp. 25–137; J. M. Miller and G. M. Tucker, *The Book of Joshua* (Cambridge: University Press, 1974), pp. 19–95.

17. For more on the "holy war" motif and its influence upon the content and structure of the narratives in Joshua 1–11, cf. G. von Rad, *Der heilige Krieg im alten Israel* (Zürich: Zwingli-Verlag, 1951); Rudolf Smend, *Yahweh War and Tribal Confederation*, trans. M. G. Rogers (Nashville: Abingdon Press, 1970); G. J. Wenham, "The Deuteronomic Theology of the Book of Joshua," *JBL* 90 (1971), 140–148.

and this time successful, attack upon 'Ai (8:3ff) is strikingly similar to those described in the account of the defeat of nearby Gibeah (Judges 20). Both stories circulated orally among the same (Benjaminite) folk population during the earliest stages of their transmission, and it is not surprising that elements of one would have been transferred to the other.[18] Finally, the account of the conquest of 'Ai provides an aetiological explanation for the prominent ruin situated southeast of Bethel (present-day Betīn). The Hebrew name *hā'ai* means "the ruin," as does the modern Arabic name of the site, "et-Tell." According to the explanation, the ruin resulted from Joshua's destruction of a massive Canaanite city which stood there at the time of the Israelite conquest (cf. especially 8:24–28). This explanation has been proven false, or at least misleading. Specifically, archaeological excavations at et-Tell have demonstrated that the massive ruins had already been standing for hundreds of years before Israel appeared on the scene.[19]

What then is the historian to make of the account? How is he to determine whether it is based on an actual historical incident? And if he decides that it is, how is he to distinguish the historically authentic elements of the account from those elements which reflect only the cultic and aetiological interests of Israel's storytellers?

It is difficult also to know what to make of the city list presented in Josh. 12:7–24 as a summary of Joshua's conquests. The city names which appear in the first part of the list correspond closely to those appearing in the preceding narratives. But not all of the cities in the list are to be accounted for in this fashion. Some of them are not associated with the conquest anywhere else in the Old Testament. Is this an artificially constructed list, either as a whole or in part? The results of one recent study strongly suggest that it is an authentic list, but that it dates from King Solomon's reign.[20]

In view of the complexity of the evidence, it is not surprising that biblical historians have reached widely divergent conclusions regarding the nature of the conquest. The three positions summarized below are representative:

18. W. M. Roth, "Hinterhalt and Scheinflucht (Der stammespolemische Hintergrund von Jos. 8)," *ZAW* 75 (1963), 296–304.

19. J. Marquet-Krause, *Les fouilles d 'Ai (et-Tell) 1933–35*, 2 vols (Paris: Libraire Orientaliste Paul Guethner, 1949). The results of Marquet-Krause's excavations have been confirmed by more recent excavations at the site (1964–69) directed by J. A. Callaway. For preliminary reports of the latter, cf. *BASOR* 178 (1965), 13–40; 196 (1969), 2–16; and 198 (1970), 7–31.

20. V. Fritz, "Die sogenannte Liste der besiegten Könige in Joshua 12," *ZDPV* 85 (1969), 136–161.

(1) The earlier commentators sought to harmonize the apparent discrepancies in the Joshua-Judges account by explaining that, while Joshua did indeed conquer the land, the individual tribes delayed for various reasons to follow up and take full possession of their assigned territories. Many contemporary scholars still hold this view in a slightly modified form.[21] Specifically, they explain that Joshua's conquest involved only certain key Canaanite royal cities. This venture weakened the system of city-states which had dominated Canaan previously and thereby opened the way for a second stage of conquest during which the individual tribes gradually gained full possession of the land. The obvious strength of this approach is that it allows for the validity of both the Deuteronomistic claim of a complete and unified military conquest and of the pre-Deuteronomistic traditions which imply a more gradual settlement of individual tribes. Archaeological evidence is also called upon in support of this approach, as summarized here by G. E. Wright:

In any view of the Conquest which we reconstruct it is now necessary to take into account two different groups of archaeological data. One group suggests a major and violent disturbance in 13th-century Palestine which brought an end to several important Canaanite cities. The other group of data is from the period of the Israelite "Judges" during the 12th and 11th centuries. It indicates that this age was one of the most disturbed and chaotic in the country's history. Every town thus far excavated was destroyed from one to four times, at least, during these two centuries. Yet, so far few of the destructions can be correlated with one another; and this suggests precisely what the Book of Judges implies: namely, that the fighting was continuous and largely local in nature.

When we put the historical and archaeological data together, we arrive at a view somewhat as follows: There was an Israelite campaign of great violence and success during the 13th century. Its purpose was to destroy the existing Canaanite city-state system, weakening local power to such an extent that new settlement, especially in the hill country, might be possible. In the centuries that followed, however, there was not only the necessity of reducing unconquered city-states but also of continuous struggle with many of the inhabitants who, though their major centres of power had been reduced, still were able to offer resistance to Israelite clans encroaching on their territory.[22]

The weakness of this approach is that it tends to gloss over the literary-critical and traditio-historical problems which arise from the biblical texts, while at the same time it deals rather loosely with the archaeological evidence. Archaeological excavations have indeed revealed that a number of Palestinian cities were destroyed violently at

21. Cf. W. F. Albright, "The Israelite Conquest of Canaan in the Light of Archaeology," *BASOR* 74 (1939), 11–23; G. E. Wright, "Epic of Conquest," *BA* 3 (1940), 25–40, and "The Literary and Historical Problem of Joshua 10 and Judges 1," *JNES* 5 (1946), 105–114; and A. J. Mattill, "Representative Universalism and the Conquest of Canaan," *CTM* 35 (1964), 8–17.
22. G. E. Wright, *Biblical Archaeology* (Philadelphia: Westminster Press, 1962²), p. 70.

the end of the Late Bronze Age (i.e., roughly during the thirteenth century). Specifically, evidences of destruction at the end of the Late Bronze Age have been uncovered at Tell deir 'Allā (biblical Succoth?), Megiddo, Beth-shean, Bethel, Gezer, Beth-shemesh, Lachish, Tell Beit Mirsim (biblical Eglon?), Tell Abu Hawam, Hazor, and Ashdod. Obviously it is tempting to attribute these destructions to Joshua. While it is quite possible that some of them were the work of Israelite tribes, to cite these destructions together as evidence of Joshua's initial *"Blitzkrieg"* conquest involves both an overextension and an oversimplification of the archaeological evidence.

First, it cannot be assumed that these Late Bronze destructions occurred in a single wave or were due to a single cause. None of the destructions can be dated precisely; and the end of the Late Bronze Age is known to have been a politically turbulent period for the Palestinian city-states, quite apart from whatever pressures the people of Israel exerted. Second, those cities which are known from archaeological excavations to have been destroyed at the end of the Late Bronze Age are for the most part not the ones which the biblical texts associate with Joshua's conquest. The two unquestionable exceptions to this statement are Lachish (Josh. 10:3ff.) and Hazor (11:1ff.). Tell Beit Mirsim is another possibility, depending upon whether it can be identified as Eglon (10:3ff.).[23] Gezer and Bethel appear in the summary list of Josh. 12:7–24. But Josh. 10:33 carefully avoids the notion that Joshua actually took the city of Gezer itself (cf. also 16:10; Judg. 1:29; 1 Kings 9:16–17); and the account of the taking of Bethel does not appear prior to the summary—as one would expect if its conquest were to be credited to Joshua—but in Judg. 1:22–26, where the deed is credited to "the house of Joseph." Actually, one need not assume that the taking of Bethel as described in Judg. 1:22–26 involved the city's destruction. Finally, archaeological excavations at the sites which do figure prominently among the conquests attributed to Joshua have, with the exception of Hazor, produced only negative evidence. The sites of Jericho and 'Ai appear to have been unoccupied during the Late Bronze Age. Gibeon may have been occupied at that time; but if so, all of the evidence except for four tombs escaped the excavators.

(2) A quite different approach to the conquest was advanced by Albrecht Alt in 1925,[24] developed by Martin Noth,[25] and finds many

23. Tell Beit Mirsim is not in any case to be identified as biblical Debir, as some still hold. Cf. most recently, Moshe Kochavi, "Khirbet Rabûd=Debir," *JTUIA* 1 (1974), 2–33.
24. A. Alt, "The Settlement of the Israelites in Palestine," *Essays on Old Testament History and Religion*, trans. R. A. Wilson (New York: Doubleday, 1967), pp. 173–221.
25. Cf. esp. M. Noth, *Das Buch Josua, HAT* 7/1 (Tübingen: J. C. B. Mohr, 1953²) and *The History of Israel*, pp. 68–84.

adherents among contemporary scholars.[26] According to this second approach, the taking of Canaan began not with a sweeping military conquest by a unified Israel, but with a gradual movement of individual tribes and clans into the thinly populated Palestinian hill country. Nor did these tribal groups come in search of permanent homes, but as nomads, or semi-nomads with small herds of cattle, who penetrated farther and farther into the land each year in their search for summer pasturage. Contacts with the Canaanite cities will have been limited at first and, except for occasional clashes, generally peaceful. This would have been the case since the Israelite tribes neither posed a serious military threat nor encroached upon the better agricultural lands of the plains. Only later, as the Israelites gradually became sedentary farmers themselves and began to combine their strength, did they enter a second stage of settlement which Alt called "territorial expansion." Basically this was an expansion from the hill country, where the tribes had by now established firm footing, into the more arable lands of the plains where the Canaanite cities generally were stronger and less widely scattered. This second stage of settlement, which did involve military conquest, was just beginning at the end of the period of the Judges and reached fruition during the reigns of David and Solomon.

Alt supported his reconstruction of the Israelite settlement/conquest with observations regarding the territorial divisions of pre-Israelite Palestine as reflected in the Egyptian sources. The most revealing sources in this regard are the campaign reports and conquest lists of Tuthmosis III (ca. 1504–1450 B.C.) and the Amarna tablets.[27] It is apparent from these sources that the typical political structure of Syria-Palestine during the Late Bronze Age was the "city-state"—i.e., the land was divided up into relatively small regions, each dominated by a fortified city with its hereditary ruler. To the extent that the pharaohs were able to exercise authority over Syria-Palestine, they did so through these local rulers. Alt observed that in the fertile Palestinian lowlands these city-states tended to be concentrated close to each other, while in the hill country they were either nonexistent or scattered far apart. Admittedly, the political situation in the Palestinian hill country cannot be reconstructed fully from the Egyptian sources. But enough evidence is available to suggest that the hill country was less

26. E.g., Manfred Weippert, *The Settlement of the Israelite Tribes in Palestine*, trans., J. D. Martin, *SBT* 21 (Naperville, Ill.: Alec R. Allenson, 1971); Siegfried Hermann, *A History of Israel in Old Testament Times*, trans. John Bowden (Philadelphia: Fortress Press, 1975), pp. 86–111.
27. Cf. Chapter I, pp. 5–6.

densely populated and tended to be divided into larger political-territorial units. Alt observed further that chains of city-states protruded into the hill country at two points, breaking it into three major divisions. A chain of city-states extended from Acco across the Jezreel Valley to Beth-shan, dividing the Galilean hill country from the central hill country. A second chain extended from the coastal plain into the hill country at approximately Jerusalem, dividing the north central (Ephraimite) from the south central (Judean) hill country. These three thinly populated and relatively isolated sections of the Palestinian hill country would have been especially vulnerable to intruders such as the Israelite tribes, in Alt's opinion, and the pre-Deuteronomistic materials in Joshua, Judges, and the opening chapters of 1 Samuel depict the Israelites struggling to gain a foothold in precisely these three areas. Thus Alt summarized his views on the Israelite settlement as follows:

. . . basically, it was the occupation of those parts of the country which already formed large political units, and continued to do so afterwards, i.e., principally the mountains, which had been only slightly affected by the spread of the city-state system. These territories, as yet ill-organized politically, and probably still thinly populated, were least capable of resisting the advance of the Israelites, and offered them the best opportunity of settling down and gradually turning from their semi-nomadic way of life to an agricultural economy. In contrast to this, the city-state system established in the plains at first encountered the Israelite occupation only at its outlying points; and only a small part of it was destroyed immediately. Its final conquest was yet to come, when the Israelite states turned wholeheartedly to a policy of political expansion, at the beginning of the first millennium B.C.[28]

Perhaps the major strength of Alt's approach is that it is grounded on those written sources which have the strongest claims to historical authenticity—i.e., the earlier pre-Deuteronomistic materials in Joshua–1 Samuel and official Egyptian records. What would be considered a major weakness of his approach by some is that it completely disregards the claims of Joshua 1–12 that Israel conquered the whole land of Canaan at the very beginning. Alt himself did not consider this a weakness, however, since he viewed the stories in Joshua 1–12 as basically folk aetiologies and rejected the Deuteronomistic concept of the conquest which dominates these chapters as ideal and historically unrealistic.[29] Alt's followers are sometimes accused of disregarding the

28. Alt, "The Settlement of the Israelites in Palestine," pp. 219–220.

29. A. Alt, "Josua," BZAW 66 (Berlin: Alfred Töpelmann, 1936), pp. 13–29; reprinted in Kleine Schriften zur Geschichte des Volkes Israel (München: C. H. Beck'sche Verlagsbuchhandlung, 1953), I, 176–192. Alt's assessment of Joshua 1–12 was developed further and modified somewhat by M. Noth. See especially the latter's Das Buch Josua, pp. 20–73.

archaeological evidence as well.[30] But this is simply not true. It would be more accurate to say that they are more cautiously aware of the limitations of the archaeological evidence for clarifying the conquest/settlement question.[31]

(3) A third position, developed primarily by G. E. Mendenhall,[32] holds that there was no conquest at all from the outside, but what might be described more accurately as a "peasants' revolt" from within. True, the revolt was probably initiated by a group of people, possibly of Palestinian origin, who had escaped slavery in Egypt; and the rebellion probably began east of the Jordan—i.e., with the kingdoms of Sihon of Heshbon and Og of Bashan—before spreading rapidly westward. But there was neither an invasion nor a significant change in population. Only the kings and nobility of the oppressive city-states were exterminated. Mendenhall rejects the idea that the Israelite tribes were nomadic or semi-nomadic in origin. He finds the key to their beginnings, rather, in the biblical designation "Hebrew" which he considers to be virtually synonymous with the 'apiru of the Amarna tablets and other ancient Near Eastern documents. The term 'apiru apparently referred to individuals or groups which stood outside the acknowledged social system for one reason or another and thus could not or did not claim the legal rights and protection which the community normally guaranteed. The nation Israel was truly "Hebrew" in origin, according to Mendenhall, since it had its roots in an open rebellion against the previously existing social system.

The fact is, and the present writer would regard it as a fact though not every detail can be "proven," that both the Amarna materials and the biblical events represent politically the same process: namely, the withdrawal, not physically and geographically, but politically and subjectively, of large population groups from any obligation to the existing political regimes, and therefore, the renunciation of any protection from those sources. In other words, there was no statistically important invasion of Palestine at the beginning of the twelve tribe system of Israel. There was no radical displacement of population, there was no genocide, there was no large scale driving out of population, only of royal administrators (of necessity!). In summary, there was no real conquest of Palestine at all; what happened instead may be termed, from the point of view of the secular

---

30. Note that Alt published his treatment of "The Settlement of the Israelites in Palestine" (1925) before enough archaeological data were available from Palestinian sites to enter significantly into the discussion of the conquest/settlement.

31. Cf. Martin Noth, "Der Beitrag der Archäologie zur Geschichte Israels," *VT Supp.* 7 (1959), 262–282; Roland de Vaux, "On the Right and Wrong Uses of Archaeology," *Near Eastern Archaeology in the Twentieth Century: Essays in Honor of Nelson Glueck*, ed. J. A. Sanders (New York: Doubleday, 1970), pp. 64–80.

32. G. E. Mendenhall, "The Hebrew Conquest of Palestine," *BA* 25 (1962), 66–87, reprinted in *The Biblical Archaeologist Reader* 3 (New York: Doubleday, 1970), 100–120; *The Tenth Generation* (Baltimore: Johns Hopkins University Press, 1973).

historian interested only in socio-political processes, a peasant's revolt against the network of interlocking Canaanite city states.[33]

Mendenhall is probing in directions which merit further research. Biblical scholars have overworked the concept of Israel's nomadic origins and all too often appealed to it uncritically. Obviously too the autochthonous population of the land of Canaan was not entirely exterminated to make room for the newcomers. They were also to contribute to the population of the later nation Israel, and the sociological process by which this occurred begs for further clarification. But the motifs of Israel's nomadic (or semi-nomadic) origins and of her entering and taking possession of the land cannot be brushed aside entirely. Both themes were too deeply engrained in her memory.[34]

THE AMPHICTYONY HYPOTHESIS

The genealogies of the Old Testament are complex constructions intended to express the geographical, ethnical, sociological, and historical interrelationships of the peoples of the ancient world. For example, some of the names which appear in these lists are clearly geographical designations (cf. especially the so-called table of nations in Genesis 10). Others are the names of the theoretical ancestors of ethnic, tribal, or national groups, and their positions in the genealogies should be taken less as biographical data than as indications of the ethnic connections and/or historical circumstances of the peoples supposedly descended from them. Thus the biblical genealogies and patriarchal sagas associate the twelve tribes of Israel with twelve forefathers, each bearing the name of his respective tribe (or vice versa), and all descended from a single patriarch named Israel (Jacob). As biographical information regarding the patriarchs, this data is of questionable validity. But it is authentic witness to a close historical bond which came to exist among the "Israelite" tribes. Moreover, the birth stories in Gen. 29:31ff. and 35:16–20 suggest that, among these tribes, some were understood to be more closely related than others—i.e., they are subdivided into six Leah tribes, two Bilhah tribes, two Zilpah tribes, and two Rachel tribes.

The number twelve appears not to be accidental. Note that the biblical genealogies indicate several other tribal (eponymous) groups which were twelve (or six) in number: twelve descendants of Nahor (Gen. 22:20–24), twelve descendants of Ishmael (25:13–16), twelve

---

33. Mendenhall, "The Hebrew Conquest of Palestine," p. 73.

34. There are also some problems with the 'apiru/Hebrew/Israel equation, upon which Mendenhall's hypothesis depends so heavily. Cf. Weippert, The Settlement of the Israelite Tribes in Palestine, pp. 63–102.

descendants of Esau (36:10–14), six descendants of Seir the Horite (36:20–28). Likewise it is significant to note that, although the actual identity of the twelve Israelite tribes varies in different passages, the number twelve itself remains constant. Compare in this regard Gen. 29:31ff.; 49; Numbers 1; 26; and Deuteronomy 33.

	Gen. 29:31ff.; 49	Num. 1; 26	Deut. 33
Leah	Reuben	Reuben	Reuben
	Simeon	Simeon	—
	Levi	—	Levi
	Judah	Judah	Judah
	Issachar	Issachar	Issachar
	Zebulun	Zebulun	Zebulun
Bilhah	Dan	Dan	Dan
	Naphtali	Naphtali	Naphtali
Zilpah	Gad	Gad	Gad
	Asher	Asher	Asher
Rachel	Joseph	Ephraim	Ephraim
	—	Manasseh	Manasseh
	Benjamin	Benjamin	Benjamin

Levi is not counted among the secular tribes in Numbers 1 and 26 (cf. also Joshua 13–21) and Simeon is absent in Deuteronomy 33. Yet the number twelve is maintained in both cases by treating Joseph as two different tribes: Ephraim and Manasseh.

Already in 1864 Heinrich Ewald observed the repeated occurrences of the number twelve in the biblical genealogies, called attention to the apparent parallel with the "amphictyonic" leagues of ancient Greece and Italy where the numbers twelve and six also tend to recur, and postulated the existence of Palestinian tribal organizations on the order of European amphictyonies.[35] The possibility was touched upon occasionally by other scholars thereafter until it received full treatment by Martin Noth in 1930.[36] Noth concluded that there was indeed an Israelite tribal confederacy during the pre-monarchical period which was structurally similar to the European amphictyonies and that more than one stage of its evolution is discernible.

The Greek verb which corresponds to the term "amphictyony" means to "dwell near" or "dwell around," and a centrally located religious shrine shared by the constituents seems to have been a standard ele-

35. H. Ewald, *Einleitung in die Geschichte des Volkes Israels*, I (Göttingen, 1864³), pp. 519 ff. Ewald did not actually use the term "amphictyony."
36. M. Noth, *Das System der zwölf Stämme Israels*, BWANT 4. Folge, 1 (Stuttgart: W. Kohlhammer, 1930). Various ramifications of the amphictyony were worked out by Noth in later studies and summarized in his *The History of Israel* (pp. 53 ff.). Cf. also *Die Gesetze im Pentateuch* (Halle: Max Niemeyer, 1940), in *The Laws in the Pentateuch and Other Essays*, trans. D. R. Ap-thomas (Edinburgh: Oliver & Boyd, 1966), pp. 1–107; and "Das Amt des 'Richters Israels'"; see note 2, Chapter IV.

ment of the European amphictyonies. Thus the best known of these amphictyonies, the Delphic League, was composed of twelve tribes associated with the temple of Apollo at Delphi.[37] Noth suggested that the recurrence of the number twelve (or six) may have had to do with the upkeep of the central shrine—i.e., each constituent group of the amphictyony would have been responsible for the upkeep one month or two months each year. Moreover, at least two factors indicated, in Noth's opinion, that Israel's twelve-tribe amphictyony evolved from an earlier six-tribe league: (1) the Leah tribes were six in number which suggests that they once constituted an autonomous amphictyony; (2) the tribes of Reuben, Simeon, and Levi appear to have lost their independent, landholding status quite early in Israel's history. Thus their listing as prominent tribes within the Leah group testifies to the antiquity of the Leah amphictyony.[38]

Noth concluded from this and other bits of evidence gleaned from the Old Testament that the Leah and concubine tribes were already settled in Canaan before the arrival of Joseph and Benjamin.[39] The Leah amphictyony was already in operation: Reuben, Simeon, and Levi occupied the central hill country west of the Jordan, and Shechem served as the central shrine. The arrival of the Joseph and Benjamin tribes resulted in a displacement of Reuben, Simeon, and Levi, and soon called for an expansion of the six-tribe league into a twelve-tribe league. A further modification occurred in the membership of the league when Levi withdrew. This allowed Joseph to be treated as two separate tribes, Ephraim and Manasseh.

Once the twelve-tribe association had been constituted on the model of the six-tribe association, the only change it underwent was caused by the withdrawal of Levi, which offered an opportunity for the tribes of Machir (Manasseh) and Ephraim to be incorporated into the system as separate units in place of the old entity of the "house of Joseph." Apart from that, no further change was made in the firmly established system, even when the composition of the tribes underwent various changes in the course of the historical development. This complicated evolution of the twelve-tribe system also explains why none of the forms that have come down to us reproduces

---

37. Actually the Delphic League possessed two shrines, the other being the temple of Demeter at Pylae. Noth believed that the Demeter temple had been the central shrine at first, but that its role was later usurped by the Apollo temple (*Das System der zwölf Stämme Israels*, pp. 47-49.)

38. Reuben and Simeon have a very shadowy existence in the biblical traditions. They are assigned territory in Joshua 13-22, but in fact do not appear to have been autonomous landholding tribes during the monarchical period. The connection between the tribe of Levi listed among the Leah tribes and the Levitical priesthood is unclear. The biblical genealogies equate the two. But it may be that the term "Levite" used in the latter context originated as an occupational designation.

39. In *Das System der zwölf Stämme Israels* (p. 66) Noth associates Benjamin with an earlier wave of settlement in the central hill country before the arrival of the Joseph group. In *The History of Israel* (p. 89) he associates their arrival with the late-comers.

the state of affairs prevailing at a particular time, since to some extent earlier organizations, to which the later elements were added, were always preserved within it. But all this merely shows that the system itself is a historical phenomenon related to a historical institution.[40]

The matter of the central shrine posed a problem for the amphictyony hypothesis from the beginning. The biblical traditions relative to the pre-monarchical period know of not one but several shrines—principally Shechem (Josh. 8:30–35; 24:1–28), Bethel (Judg. 20:18), Shiloh (1 Sam. 1ff.), and Gilgal (Josh. 4:19ff.; 1 Sam. 10:8; 13:8–15; 15:12–21). In response to this problem Noth postulated that the ark was the symbol of Israel's tribal unity more so than the shrine which housed it, and that the ark was in fact transferred occasionally from one shrine to another. Shechem had been the center of the earlier six-tribe amphictyony, in Noth's opinion, and he cautiously raised the possibility that the account of the ceremony in Josh. 24:1–28 actually harks back to that historical moment when the Leah tribes, the concubine tribes, Joseph, and Benjamin bound themselves together into a twelve-tribe league. Since it was the Joseph group which introduced both Yahwism and the ark into Palestine, in his opinion, this would have been for the remaining tribes quite literally a moment of putting away the gods of the land in deference to Yahweh (Josh. 24:14ff.). Later, for some unknown reason, the ark would have been transferred to Bethel, making it the central shrine. Later still the ark was moved to Gilgal, and finally to Shiloh where it remained until its capture by the Philistines.

Noth proceeded then, using the European amphictyonies as a model, to clarify and fill in further the picture of Israel's tribal organization during the pre-monarchical period. The member tribes of the confederation will have had official representation corresponding to the *hieromnemones* of the Greek amphictyonies. Perhaps this was the role of the *nᵉsiʾim* ("princes" or "leaders") to which several Old Testament passages refer (cf. especially Num. 1:5–16; 2:7). There must have been legal regulations associated with the league and officials to oversee their observance. Noth argued that a deposit of this amphictyonic law is preserved in parts of the book of the Covenant (Exodus 21–23), and that the "minor judges" listed in Judg. 10:1–5; 12:7–15 held office as legal authorities over the league. There will have been periodic cultic festivals held at the central sanctuary at which the amphictyonic bond was reaffirmed and the council of *nᵉsiʾim* discussed matters of concern. Occasionally too the tribes will have joined together in warfare. But

40. Noth, *The History of Israel*, p. 90.

these were primarily defensive wars, in Noth's opinion, or wars conducted against member tribes of the amphictyony who had transgressed the amphictyonic regulations in some way (cf., e.g., Judges 19–21).

Although Noth's conclusions and proposals were never accepted in full by all biblical scholars, his research resulted in a general recognition that Israel was organized into an amphictyony of some sort during the period of the Judges. Indeed, it soon became common practice to refer to the period of the Judges as "the amphictyonic period," and the amphictyony hypothesis served as a catalyst and presupposition for numerous secondary hypotheses which have affected research in virtually every area of Old Testament studies.[41] However, the amphictyony hypothesis has fallen under increasing attack, beginning in the 1960's, especially with an article by H. M. Orlinsky.[42] There are basically two objections: (1) The European amphictyonies were remote chronologically, geographically, and culturally from early Israel, and there appears to be much less real evidence for a parallel between the two than earlier supposed. (2) The use of the amphictyonic model for "clarifying" and "filling out" the scanty evidence available for Israel's pre-monarchical period has resulted in artificial constructions which find little or no support in the biblical texts themselves.

As it turns out, the European amphictyonies were far less homogeneous than earlier supposed; generally they were leagues of city-states rather than of tribal groups; and the numbers twelve and six were by no means standard. Twelve seems to function as a symbolic number in the Old Testament, on the other hand, and as such may well have been superimposed upon Israel's early traditions.

If the number twelve was not standard for the amphictyonies and is more symbolic than historical in the Old Testament, then Noth's reconstruction of the stages by which Israel's supposed amphictyony developed from a six-tribe league into a twelve-tribe league is of questionable validity. In any case, the presumption of a well-organized tribal league around a central sanctuary—even if we allow for several

41. On the far-reaching influence of the amphictyony hypothesis in recent Old Testament research, cf. Georg Fohrer, "Altes Testament—'Amphiktyonie' und 'Bund'?" ThLZ 91 (1966), 801–816, 893–904; and John Hayes. "The Twelve-Tribe Amphictyony: An Appraisal," Trinity University Studies in Religion 10 (1975), pp. 22–36, first presented in 1972.
42. H. M. Orlinsky, "The Tribal System of Israel and Related Groups in the Period of the Judges," OA 1 (1962), 11–20; W. H. Irwin, "Le sanctuaire central israélite avant l'éstablissement de la monarchie," RB 72 (1965), 161–184; G. Fohrer, "Altes Testament—'Amphiktyonie' und 'Bund'?"; G. W. Anderson, "Israel; Amphictyony; 'am; ḳāhāl; 'ēdâh," Translating and Understanding the Old Testament, ed. H. T. Frank and W. L. Reed (New York: Abingdon Press, 1970), pp. 135–151; R. de Vaux, "La Thèse de la' 'amphictyonie Israélite,' " HTR 64 (1971), 415–436; J. Hayes, "The Twelve-Tribe Amphictyony: An Appraisal"; A. D. H. Mayes, Israel in the Period of the Judges, SBT, second series, 29 (Naperville, Ill.: Alec R. Allenson, 1974).

different central sanctuaries in sequence—conflicts with the impression one receives from the narratives collected in the book of Judges. This was Orlinsky's chief objection:

In reading this book, one is struck time and again by several outstanding facts, which together help to make up a pretty clear and consistent pattern of tribal affiliation—or lack of it. The facts are these. The "Judges" . . . were individual men who exhibited unusual military or physical prowess in time of dire circumstances for their kinfolk, leading them in victory over threatening non-Israelite invaders or in overthrowing the yoke of an enemy. Ehud of the tribe of Benjamin, Shamgar ben Anath, and Jephthah the son of a prostitute are cases in point. These military chieftains . . . were not associated with any shrines. And none of them was an amphictyon. ·

It is significant, further, that no amphictyonic league ever met at a shrine to decide a course of action or to pick a "Judge." One will go through all twenty-one chapters of the book of Judges and fail to find mention of Shiloh, or Shechem, or Bethel, or Ramah, or Beth-shean, or Gilgal, or any other shrine, at which a confederacy of two, or six, or twelve, or any number of tribes met as an amphictyony.[43]

Noth could point, of course, to Josh. 24:1–28 as an example of an amphictyonic assembly at a central sanctuary. But even he was very · cautious at this point since, at least in their present forms, both this passage and the closely related Josh. 8:30–35 are clearly late Deuteronomistic formulations. Possibly these two passages are based on old authentic tradition. But neither can this be established with certainty nor can the supposed old tradition be reconstructed with confidence. A similar situation exists with regard to the $n^e si'im$. It is not farfetched to suppose that these were tribal representatives of the amphictyony, presuming that the existence of an amphictyony can be established on other grounds. But one would expect to find at least a few references to the $n^e si'im$ in their capacity as tribal representatives in the stories of the book of Judges if they really played such a role at that time. On the contrary, the term is confined almost entirely to the later strata of the Old Testament.

The situation which has occurred with regard to the amphictyony hypothesis illustrates very well the ongoing process of historical research. As the historian works through the available sources from the past he develops hypotheses and reconstructions which he believes best explain these sources. Those hypotheses and reconstructions which survive the scrutiny of other (contemporary and later) historians become the "historical facts." No historian expects all of his conclusions to survive, and he is well aware that those which do will probably be

43. Orlinsky, "The Tribal System of Israel," pp. 12–14.

modified by others. Above all, he knows that all historical facts, even those which he may have helped to create and holds most dear, are subject to repeal at any time, due to new findings or the results of further research. One can safely predict a lively discussion of the amphictyony hypothesis over the next few years. If it is found in the final analysis to be unconvincing, many of the related conclusions reached by historians since the 1930's will have to be carefully reconsidered and retested also to see whether they can stand on their own without the support of the amphictyonic model.

V

Establishing a Chronological Framework

The historian cannot be content with simply recounting past events at random. Historical events do not occur at random, but always in relationship to preceding events and surrounding circumstances. This means, in short, that the historian must make every effort to establish an accurate chronological framework for the period under investigation. Unfortunately, the matter of chronology presents the historian of Old Testament times with some perplexing problems. We have already touched upon some of these problems but the matter requires further attention still.

First a word about Israel's history in context. Appendix I provides an outline of the archaeological periods of Syria-Palestine with approximate dates and some correlations with the general features of ancient Near Eastern history. From the perspective of such an outline it can be seen that the nation Israel was a late-comer to the scene. Israel was one of several medium-sized kingdoms which arose in Mesopotamia and Syria-Palestine during the early part of the Iron Age and existed independently for a time before being engulfed by a succession of larger empires (Assyria, Babylon, Persia, Macedonia, Rome). The various tribal groups which were to constitute Israel had their origin in the Bronze Age. And Judah emerged again during the Hellenistic period as an independent kingdom for approximately a century (166–63 B.C.). But the Israel of the Old Testament belongs essentially to the Iron Age.

THE CHRONOLOGICAL FRAMEWORK OF GENESIS–2 KINGS

The Old Testament itself reflects a strong interest in chronology, as is indicated by the numerous chronological notations scattered throughout the so-called historical books and certain of the prophetical books, especially Jeremiah, Ezekiel, Haggai, and Zechariah. Moreover, there emerges from the chronological data presented in Genesis–2

70

Kings a rather precise chronological framework which extends in coverage from Creation to the Exile.

The period from Adam to Abraham is covered by the genealogies in Genesis 5 and 11:10–32. Since these are unilinear genealogies which trace lineage always from father to oldest son and indicate in each case the father's age at the birth of his oldest son, one can calculate the number of years which transpired between Creation and each new generation.

When Adam had lived a hundred and thirty years, he became the father of a son . . . , and named him Seth. [=*Anno Mundi* 130]

. . . .

When Seth had lived a hundred and five years, he became the father of Enosh. [=A.M. 235]

. . . .

When Enosh had lived ninety years, he became the father of Kenan. [=A.M. 325]

Corresponding figures for Abraham, Isaac, and Jacob are provided in Gen. 21:5; 25:7, 26; 35:28, and 47:28, which place their respective births at A.M. 1946, A.M. 2046, and A.M. 2106. Gen. 47:9 indicates that Jacob entered Egypt with his family in his 130th year (=A.M. 2236), Ex. 12:40 places the Exodus from Egypt 430 years later (=A.M. 2666), and 1 Kings 6:1 dates Solomon's founding of the temple in his fourth year and 480 years after the Exodus (=A.M. 3146). Chronological coverage from Solomon to the Exile is provided then by the regnal period reckonings recorded in 1–2 Kings for the rulers of the Divided Kingdoms. We are told that Solomon reigned forty years (1 Kings 11:42), which would place Rehoboam's accession to the throne of Judah thirty-seven years after the founding of the temple (=A.M. 3183). Rehoboam reigned seventeen years (1 Kings 14:21), placing Abijah's accession in A.M. 3200; Abijah reigned three years (1 Kings 15:2), placing Asa's accession in A.M. 3203, etc.

This chronological framework which emerges from Genesis–2 Kings should greatly simplify the biblical historian's task. That is, it would seem theoretically possible, with a few further computations, to restate the biblical chronological figures in terms of the Julian calendar and to correlate them with dates available from non-biblical sources. Indeed this was the procedure followed in the seventeenth century by Archbishop James Ussher, whose computations were incorporated into the notes of the King James version of the Bible. Upon closer examination, however, one finds that the biblical figures do not submit willingly to such an approach. Even Archbishop Ussher was forced to

71

be somewhat selective in his use of the biblical data and arbitrary in his computations.[1]

There are basically four complicating factors: (1) The different manuscript traditions preserve variant readings which significantly affect the chronology of Genesis–2 Kings. The example figures quoted above are those of the Masoretic tradition which serves as the basis of most modern language translations of the Old Testament but does not always preserve the most authentic readings.[2] (2) The chronological framework outlined above is in conflict at several points with other chronological data presented in Genesis–2 Kings. (3) It is in striking conflict as well with chronological data available from non-biblical sources. (4) This chronological framework reflects the influence of theoretical and schematic concepts of history which were popular during ancient times but which the present-day historian must view with suspicion. Following are some examples of each of these complicating factors:

(1) The Masoretic tradition, the Samaritan Pentateuch, and the major Septuagint manuscripts present three different sets of chronological figures for the pre-patriarchal ancestors in Genesis 5 and 11:10–32.[3] We observed above that the Masoretic figures imply a date of A.M. 1946 for Abraham's birth, which would mean that his migration from Haran to Canaan (occurring during his seventy-fifth year, Gen. 12:4) would be dated A.M. 2021. Calculating with the figures preserved for Genesis 5 and 11:10–32 by the Samaritan Pentateuch, however, one arrives at the dates A.M. 2247 and A.M. 2322 for Abraham's birth and migration, or with the Septuagint figures, A.M. 3312 and A.M. 3387.

The date of Abraham's migration to Canaan becomes crucial when another textual variation is taken into account. According to the Masoretic rendition of Ex. 12:40, "the time that the people of Israel dwelt in Egypt was four hundred and thirty years." One naturally assumes from this reading that the Exodus is to be placed 430 years after Jacob's entrance into Egypt (i.e., A.M. 2666). But the same verse as rendered by the Samaritan Pentateuch and the Septuagint indicates

1. E.g., Ussher depended primarily upon the figures provided by the Masoretic tradition, but followed the Septuagint (=Samaritan Pentateuch) version of Ex. 12:40. See below.
2. We observed in Chapter II, for example, that the pattern of synchronisms preserved in the Lucianic recension of the Septuagint for the rulers of the Omride period have a stronger claim to authenticity than the Masoretic pattern (see pp. 37–38). For a helpful discussion of the various manuscript traditions, cf. R. W. Klein, *Textual Criticism of the Old Testament* (Philadelphia: Fortress Press, 1975).
3. Cf. the tabulation of this data prepared by M. D. Johnson, *The Purpose of the Biblical Genealogies* (Cambridge: University Press, 1969), app. 2, pp. 262–263.

that the 430 years covered the period of sojournings ". . . *in the land
of Canaan and* in the land of Egypt." This would mean that the 430-
year period began not with Jacob's entrance into Egypt but with
Abraham's entrance into Canaan. Correspondingly, the Exodus would
be dated A.M. 2451 with the Masoretic figures, A.M. 2752 with the
Samaritan Pentateuch figures, or A.M. 3817 with the Septuagint figures.
Both Saint Paul and Josephus knew the version of Ex. 12:40 preserved
in the Samaritan Pentateuch and the Septuagint. Thus Paul placed the
coming of the law 430 years after the promises to Abraham (Gal.
3:15–18). And Josephus tells us that the Hebrews ". . . left Egypt in
the months of Xanthicus, on the fifteenth by lunar reckoning, 430 years
after the coming of our forefather Abraham to Canaan, Jacob's migration to Egypt having taken place 215 years later."[4]

The Septuagint manuscripts depart from the Masoretic tradition
again in 1 Kings 6:1 where they place Solomon's founding of the
temple 440 years (as compared to 480 years) after the Exodus. Some
of the Septuagint manuscripts preserve different figures for the lengths
of the reigns of Abijah and Jehoram of Judah (1 Kings 15:2; 2 Kings
8:17).

(2) The chronological notation in 1 Kings 6:1 which places the
founding of the temple 480 years (440 years according to the Septuagint) after the Exodus conflicts with other chronological data
presented in the Genesis–2 Kings corpus requiring a longer interval of
time. Specifically, Num. 14:33–34 states that the Israelites wandered in
the wilderness for forty years after their escape from Egypt; chronological data presented in the books of Judges–2 Samuel require another
490 years for the period of the Judges and David's reign (Judg. 3:8,
11, 14, 30, etc.),[5] and to this must be added some time for the careers
of Joshua, Samuel, and Saul[6] as well as the first four years of Solomon's
reign.

Other conflicts occur between the regnal period reckonings and
synchronisms recorded for the rulers of the Divided Kingdoms—i.e.,
occasionally a king is attributed a longer or shorter reign than the
associated synchronisms allow. Compare, for example, the figures
recorded for Jehoahaz of Israel.

4. *Jewish Antiquities* II. 15.2, trans. H. St. J. Thackeray, *The Loeb Classical Library: Josephus,*
vol. IV (London: William Heinemann, 1926), pp. 304–305. Cf. also I. 6.5 and X. 8.4–5 (*Loeb
Library* ed., vol. IV, pp. 72–77 and vol. VI, pp. 234–237).
5. Cf. the tabulation prepared by C. F. Burney, *The Book of Judges* (London: Rivingtons, 1918),
pp. i–li.
6. No chronological data are recorded for the careers of Joshua and Samuel. 1 Sam. 13:1 probably indicated a twenty-year reign for Saul but the text is now corrupt.

73

In the twenty-third year of Joash the son of Ahaziah king of Judah, Jehoahaz the son of Jehu began to reign over Israel in Samaria, and he reigned seventeen years.

. . . .

In the thirty-seventh year of Joash king of Judah Jehoash the son of Jehoahaz began to reign over Israel in Samaria . . . (2 Kings 13:1, 10)

If Jehoahaz's reign began during Joash's twenty-third year and ended before or during Joash's thirty-seventh year, how then could it have lasted more than fifteen years? Yet his regnal period is reckoned at seventeen years. Similar conflicts emerge, as we have seen, from the chronological data recorded for the rulers of the Omride period. Compare also the data recorded for Uzziah of Judah (= Azariah, 2 Kings 15:1f.) and Hoshea of Israel (2 Kings 17:1).[7]

(3) The most striking conflict between the chronological framework of Genesis–2 Kings and chronological data available from non-biblical sources has to do with the age of the earth and the beginnings of human civilization. Calculations on the basis of the biblical figures will vary somewhat depending upon the textual tradition favored, but will lead in any case to a date not far from 4000 B.C. for Creation and Adam's first year. Archbishop Ussher calculated Creation to have occurred 4004 B.C. Obviously such a date is not in keeping with geological evidence regarding the age of the earth. Neither is it in keeping with archaeological evidence which indicates that human occupation of the earth goes back two million years or more.

Another conflict between biblical and non-biblical chronology occurs in that the regnal periods recorded for the Hebrew kings require more time than is allowed by dates which can be established with the Mesopotamian documents. For example, the regnal periods recorded for the Israelite kings from Jehu to the fall of Samaria total 143 years, while the regnal periods recorded for the Judean rulers from Athaliah to the surrender of Jerusalem during Jehoiachin's reign total 287 years.[8] Yet

7. Some of the discrepancies associated with the synchronisms and regnal period reckonings may have quite legitimate explanations. We have already noted, for example, that the apparent discrepancies could occur if more than one kind of calendar and/or method of reckoning the beginnings and lengths of reigns were employed (Chapter II, p. 36). But certainly not all of the discrepancies are to be explained away in this fashion.

8. The overall total of years required by the regnal period reckonings can be reduced by positing occasional coregencies and presuming that some of the regnal periods recorded overlapped. But there are at least three problems with this procedure: (1) Several coregencies would be required to bring the biblical figures into line, yet the corresponding narrative accounts are silent regarding coregencies with one *possible* exception—i.e., 2 Kings 15:5 states that, since Uzziah was a leper, ". . . he dwelt in a separate house. And Jotham the king's son was over the household, governing the people of the land." (2) Although 2 Kings 15:5 can be interpreted to imply that Jotham enjoyed the status of a coregent during Uzziah's reign, the wording of verses 15:6–7 and 32–33 seem nevertheless to specify that the sixteen-year regnal period ascribed to Jotham pertained to his own individual reign following Uzziah's death. (3) The total of the regnal periods ascribed to the kings of Judah *when added in sequence* has significance for a schematic view of Israel's history which is worked out in the chronological framework of Genesis–2 Kings (see below).

74

it can be established with the Mesopotamian documents that (1) Jehu's rebellion which brought Jehu and Athaliah to the thrones of their respective kingdoms occurred no more than a year or two before 841 B.C.;[9] (2) Samaria fell approximately 722 B.C., and probably in that year;[10] and (3) the surrender of Jerusalem occurred on March 16, 597 B.C.[11] In other words, only approximately 120 years (compared with 143 years implied by the regnal period reckonings) elapsed between Jehu's seizure of the throne of Israel and the fall of Samaria; and only approximately 245 years (compared with 287 years) elapsed between Athaliah's seizure of the throne of Judah and the surrender of Jerusalem.

(4) The genealogies of Genesis 5 and 11:10–32 belong to the Priestly stratum of the Pentateuch, which means that they are to be associated roughly with the period of the Babylonian Exile. One of the notable characteristics of these genealogies is that they are cast in a literary form strikingly similar to that of the *Sumerian King List*, a Mesopotamian document which seeks to establish the order of throne succession of the early Sumerian kings.[12] The Priestly genealogies and the *Sumerian King List* also share the concept of a pre-flood golden age during which people lived (and kings reigned) for fantastically long periods of time. Thus the *Sumerian King List* credits the pre-flood kings with reigns from 10,800 to 64,800 years in length, while the Priestly Writer records life spans of generally more than nine hundred years for the pre-flood ancestors. Apparently the flood was understood to have introduced a second age during which life spans (and regnal periods) were greatly reduced but still amazingly long. The *Sumerian King List* records regnal periods of up to 1,560 years for the early post-flood kings. The Priestly Writer records life spans ranging from 148 to 600 years for the early post-flood ancestors. There is no way of knowing where the Priestly Writer or the compilers of the *Sumerian King List* derived their figures. But the critical historian must regard these figures with suspicion in any case since they correspond to a theoretical view of history, the concept of an ancient golden age, rather than to normal human experience.

Some of the other chronological figures provided in Genesis–2 Kings

9. Cf. Chapter II, p. 24; and Appendix II, item (1).
10. Cf. Appendix II, item (4).
11. Cf. Chapter I, p. 9; and Appendix II, item (7).
12. For the text of the king list see Thorkild Jacobsen, ed., *The Sumerian King List* (*Assyriological Studies* 11; Chicago: University of Chicago Press, 1939), and *ANET*, pp. 265–266. For the relationship between the priestly genealogy and the king list see J. M. Miller, "In the 'Image' and 'Likeness' of God," *JBL* 91 (1972), 289–304, esp. n. 20; and "The Descendents of Cain: Notes on Genesis 4," *ZAW* 86 (1974), 164–174, esp. n. 30.

appear also to have been influenced by theoretical speculation. We have observed, for example, that the Masoretic figures imply a date of A.M. 2666 for the Israelite Exodus from Egypt. 2666 corresponds to 26⅔ generations of one hundred years each, or to two-thirds of a Great Year of 4000 years.[13] This might seem coincidental if it were not for the fact that Aaron represents exactly the twenty-sixth generation from Adam; the remaining two-thirds generation being that of Eleazer, Aaron's son, who participaed in the Exodus. Counting forward with the Masoretic figures on the other hand, and with chronological data which would have been available to the post-Exilic Jewish community, one arrives at A.M. 4000 as the date of the rededication of the second temple following the Maccabean rebellion. 1 Kings 6:1 indicates an interval of 480 years between the Exodus and the founding of the temple during the fourth year of Solomon's reign (= A.M. 3146). The remaining years of Solomon's forty-year reign (1 Kings 11:42), plus the total of the regnal periods recorded for the kings of Judah from Solomon to the Exile (added *in sequence*), plus fifty years for the Exile[14] amounts to another 480 years (= A.M. 3626). From 538 B.C., Cyrus' first year of Babylonian rule at which time a group of exiles are said to have returned and dedicated an altar in Jerusalem (2 Chron. 36:22; Ez. 1:1ff.; 3:1ff.), to the Maccabean rededication of the second temple in 164 B.C. (1 Macc. 4:36–61) is 374 years, exactly the number required to bring the date to A.M. 4000. In short, the chronological framework of Genesis–2 Kings as preserved in the Masoretic tradition appears to have been carefully designed to emphasize four pivotal points in Israel's cultic history: the Exodus, supposedly occurring at the end of two-thirds of a Great Year of 4000 years; Solomon's founding of the first temple 480 years later; the end of the Exile and dedication of an altar in Jerusalem after another 480-year era; and the Maccabean rededication of the second temple which ended the first Great Year of 4000 years.

The preceding examples focus intentionally on the problematic features of the chronological framework in Genesis–2 Kings. The fact

---

13. Regarding this 4000-year scheme cf. J. Wellhausen, *Prolegomena to the History of Ancient Israel* (New York: Meridian, 1957), pp. 308–309; G. von Rad, *Genesis*, trans. J. H. Marks (Philadelphia: Westminster Press, 1961), p. 67; M. D. Johnson, *The Purpose of the Biblical Genealogies, Society for New Testament Studies Monograph Series* 8 (Cambridge: Cambridge University Press, 1969), pp. 32–36. For a slightly different analysis but along the same lines, cf. W. R. Windfall, "The Chronology of the Divided Monarchy of Israel," *ZAW* 80 (1968), 319–337.

14. The length of the Exile is not actually given; and in fact the period from the final fall of Jerusalem to Cyrus' decree was probably slightly less than fifty years (either forty-eight or forty-nine years). But fifty years would have been the nearest round number, and it seems to have been intended by the biblical chronologers that the era extending from the Exodus to Solomon's founding of the temple should correspond in length to the era extending from the founding of the temple to the end of the Exile.

that there are problems does not mean that all of the chronological data presented in connection with the framework are to be ignored by the historian. Some of the figures are no doubt authentic in origin and essentially correct. But it does mean that neither the framework as a whole nor its component parts can be relied upon uncritically or as a chronological standard. Among the component parts, the regnal period reckonings recorded for the rulers of the Divided Kingdoms probably have the strongest claim to authenticity. We suggested earlier that these reckonings, along with the synchronisms, may have been calculated originally on the basis of data which was derived ultimately from official court records. But as they stand now these regnal period reckonings appear to be excessively long. One possible explanation is that they were adjusted intentionally in order to accord with the schematic view of Israel's cultic history which pervades the framework as a whole. That is, the post-Exilic chronologers may have found it necessary to expand some of the regnal periods in order to achieve the 480-year era which they believed to have extended from Solomon's founding of the temple to the end of the Exile.

OTHER AVAILABLE DATA AND PROBLEM AREAS

The purpose of this concluding section is to summarize the various data available for reconstructing a chronological framework of Israel's history, and to point out some of the issues which divide scholarly opinion.

The Patriarchs: We have already explored the issues involved in dating the "Patriarchal Age" and observed that the prior question is whether the patriarchal narratives actually refer to a particular historical period (pp. 50–55). Those scholars who are convinced that they do place the patriarchs in the Bronze Age, either during the early second millennium B.C.[15] or during the Late Bronze Age. Those who favor an early second millennium date can claim some support from the chronological framework of Genesis–2 Kings, but generally recognize that this is weak support and seek to ground their case on archaeological considerations and cultural parallels. Those who favor a Late Bronze Age date for the patriarchs are influenced by the current tendency to place the Exodus as late as the thirteenth century B.C. (See below.)

The Egyptian Experience and the Exodus: Many of the same questions must be raised on literary-critical and form-critical grounds

---

15. I.e., during the EB-MB Transition and/or MB IIA ages. See Appendix I.

regarding the historicity of the biblical narratives describing the Egyptian bondage and the Exodus that were raised regarding the patriarchal narratives. Most scholars agree that only certain ones of the Israelite tribes will have participated in the Egyptian experience in any case, and some have argued strongly that there may have been more than one Exodus involving different tribal groups. Uncertainties regarding such matters warn against assigning precise dates to the Egyptian experience.[16]

Traditionally (as early as Josephus) the Israelite entrance into Egypt, their bondage there, and the Exodus have been associated with the period of Hyksos rule in Egypt and the subsequent expulsion of the Hyksos by the Eighteenth Dynasty. This would be roughly in keeping with the chronological framework in Genesis–2 Kings (Masoretic tradition) which places the Exodus in A.M. 2666 (=roughly 1500 B.C.)[17] But other biblical and non-biblical evidence strongly suggests a later date for the Exodus.

Following the discovery of the Amarna letters (1887) and throughout the 1950's, a number of biblical scholars favored a somewhat later (mid-fifteenth-century) date for the Exodus. The Amarna letters testify to the existence of 'apiru in Palestine during the fourteenth century; these 'apiru were equated with the Hebrews; and excavations at the site of ancient Jericho uncovered what was thought to be evidence of a cataclysmic destruction of the city walls approximately 1400 B.C. More recent excavations at Jericho have proven this earlier conclusion incorrect, however, while scholars have become increasingly doubtful that there is any direct connection between the 'apiru and the Hebrews. The tendency among more recent scholars, therefore, who are willing to assign a date to the Exodus at all, has been to place it in the thirteenth century. They do so for essentially three reasons: (1) Pithom and Raamses, the two Egyptian cities of bondage mentioned in Ex. 1:11, are almost certainly to be identified as cities of Ramses II (ca. 1304–1237 B.C.).[18] (2) The victory stele of Ramses' successor, Merneptah (ca. 1236–1223 B.C.), provides the earliest certain non-biblical evidence of the existence of "Israel" in Palestine. (3) Both

16. For earlier treatments of the historical and chronological issues associated with the Egyptian experience and the Exodus see especially L. B. Paton, "Israel's Conquest of Canaan," *JBL* 32 (1913), 1–53; and H. H. Rowley, *From Joseph to Joshua* (London: Oxford University Press, 1950). Two recent studies of special importance are: Siegfried Herrmann, *Israel in Egypt*, trans. Margaret Kohl, *SBT*, second series, 27 (London: SCM Press, 1974); and E. W. Nicholson, *Exodus and Sinai in History and Tradition* (Atlanta: John Knox Press, 1974).

17. I.e., using as fixed points in the Julian calendar the date of the final fall of Jerusalem (586 B.C.) and the date of Cyrus' decree (538 B.C.). See below.

18. Cf. most recently, E. P. Uphill, "Pithom and Raamses: Their Location and Signification," *JNES* 27 (1968), 291–316; 28 (1969), 15–39.

the Egyptian records and Palestinian archaeological remains indicate that the end of the Late Bronze Age and the beginning of the Iron Age were an extremely turbulent time, which would have provided reasonable circumstances for a band of Hebrews to escape Egypt and gain a foothold in Palestine.

The Period of the Judges: The important role which the Philistines, Moabites, and others play in the narratives of Judges–1 Samuel indicates the early centuries of the Iron Age as the historical context of the period of the Judges; and the establishment of the Hebrew monarchy which brought the period of the Judges to an end can be dated roughly 1000 B.C. (See below.) Otherwise, none of the individual judges can be dated with any degree of confidence. In fact, the narratives relating their deeds do not even appear to be arranged in historical order. The chronological notations scattered throughout the book of Judges belong entirely to the Deuteronomistic editorial transitions between the narratives and consist largely of estimates in round numbers. Note in this regard the constant recurrence of the numbers twenty, forty, and eighty.[19]

Judg. 3:11	Othniel's deliverance was followed by forty years of peace.
Judg. 3:30	Ehud's deliverance was followed by eighty years of peace
Judg. 4:3	Jabin oppressed Israel twenty years.
Judg. 5:31	Deborah's deliverance was followed by forty years of peace.
Judg. 8:28	Gideon's deliverance was followed by forty years of peace.
Judg. 13:1	The Philistines oppressed Israel forty years.
Judg. 15:20; 16:31	Samson judged Israel twenty plus twenty years.
1 Sam. 4:18	Eli judged Israel forty years.

The United Monarchy: The division of the United Monarchy into two kingdoms following Solomon's death is probably to be dated approximately 925–920 B.C. (see below and Appendix III), and David and Solomon are ascribed regnal periods of forty years each. Here again these forty-year regnal periods should not be taken as exact reckonings, but if one uses them as a guide this would place the beginning of Solomon's reign approximately 965–960 B.C., and the beginning of David's reign soon before 1000 B.C. Josephus may provide some confirmation in Solomon's case, if he is not himself dependent ultimately upon the biblical figures. Josephus associates the founding of the temple (Solomon's fourth regnal year) with the eleventh/twelfth year

19. It is generally recognized that the numbers twenty (=half of forty), forty, and multiples of forty function as round (and sometimes symbolic) numbers in the biblical materials.

of Hiram of Tyre. M. B. Rowton, working with the Tyrian king list (also provided by Josephus) and with known Assyrian synchronisms, arrived at 959 B.C. as the date of the event. This would place Solomon's accession approximately 962 B.C.[20]

The Period of the Divided Kingdoms: Historians must depend primarily upon the regnal period reckonings and synchronisms recorded in 1–2 Kings for the relative chronology of the rulers of the Divided Kingdoms. These figures are particularly tantalizing, as we have already seen. On the one hand there is reason to believe that they derive ultimately from official court records. On the other hand these figures are inconsistent both internally and in relation to chronological data which can be derived from the Mesopotamian documents. The occasional correlations which can be made between the reigns of the Hebrew kings and those of the Mesopotomian rulers are crucial, moreover, since the latter can be assigned absolute dates in terms of the Julian calendar.[21] The most important of these correlations for purposes of the chronology of the period of the Divided Kingdoms are summarized in Appendix II.

Two possible ways of dealing with the regnal period reckonings and synchronisms were outlined in Chapter II. One approach assumes a high degree of accuracy for the Masoretic figures and insists that the apparent conflicts are but clues to certain extenuating circumstances not actually spelled out in the biblical texts—i.e., occasional coregencies, different calendars used by the two kingdoms and different methods of reckoning the beginnings and lengths of reigns, changes in the calendars and reckoning methods from time to time.[22] In accordance with this approach one explores the different possibilities until a combination of coregencies, calendars, and reckoning methods is found which will explain the biblical figures in their present state. Once a successful combination is discovered it is taken as evidence of the accuracy of the biblical figures and used to calculate precise dates for the Hebrew kings. Two fallacies of this approach are that it involves circular argumentation and fails to take into account changes which have occurred in the biblical figures during the process of their transmission from ancient times to the present. The Masoretic figures

---

20. Josephus, *Against Apion* I. 126 (*Loeb Library* ed., vol. I, pp. 212–213) and *Jewish Antiquities* VIII. 62 (*Loeb Library* ed., vol. V, pp. 604–605); M. B. Rowton, "The Date of the Founding of Solomon's Temple," *BASOR* 119 (1950), 20–22. But see also H. J. Katzenstein, "Is There Any Synchronism between the Reigns of Hiram and Solomon?" *JNES* 24 (1965), 116–117.

21. The Assyrian kings can be dated on the basis of the *limmu* lists (see Chapter I, pp. 8–9). For the Neo-Babylonian kings see R. A. Parker and W. H. Dubberstein, *Babylonian Chronology 626 B.C.–A.D. 75* (Providence: Brown University Press, 1956).

22. See works cited in Chapter II, note 16.

in particular show evidence of having been adjusted secondarily. We saw that the Masoretic synchronisms for the rulers of the Omride period have been revised in order to accommodate the misleading chronological implications of the narrative in 2 Kings 3:4–27. Also, the regnal period reckonings appear to have been expanded, possibly in order to accommodate the schematic view of Israel's cultic history which called for a 480-year era between the founding of the temple and the Exile. Other changes may have occurred as well.

The other approach recognizes that the biblical figures are essentially authentic in origin and that some of the apparent conflicts which they present may have to do with calendars, reckoning systems, and the like. In view of the textual complexities, however, it suspects that some of the conflicts are due to the fact that the biblical figures are no longer entirely accurate. They are therefore to be followed as closely as possible. But occasionally, when indicated by other strong chronological evidence or by simple arithmetic, one must depart from them. Appendix III summarizes a chronological reconstruction of the period of the Divided Kingdoms worked out by W. F. Albright in 1945 in accordance with this second approach.[23] Dates established in accordance with this procedure are to be considered approximate and tentative. The only date which Albright considered absolutely certain was that of the fall of Samaria in 722 B.C. Some of the others (in italics) he considered to be accurate within a year or two. Most of the remainder he considered correct within five years. Two developments since 1945 call for slight modifications in Albright's dates: we have learned that the Lucianic synchronisms for the Omride period have a stronger claim to authenticity than the corresponding Masoretic synchronisms; and the first surrender of Jerusalem to Babylon can now be dated 597 B.C. rather than 596 B.C. The modifications suggested by these developments are placed in brackets.[24]

The Last Days of Jerusalem and the Exile: 2 Kings, Jeremiah, and Ezekiel date some of the events associated with the final fall of Jerusalem and the Exile to the month and day of Zedekiah's reign (= the month and day of Jehoiachin's exile), and occasionally indicate the corresponding regnal years of the Babylonian rulers (Nebuchadnezzar and Amel-Marduk). We are informed, for example, that the Babylonian captain who was to take charge of the destruction of Jerusalem

23. W. F. Albright, "The Chronology of the Divided Monarchy of Israel," *BASOR* 100 (1945), 16–22.

24. The suggested modifications associated with the Lucianic synchronisms are worked out in Miller, "Another Look at the Chronology of the Early Divided Monarchy," *JBL* 86 (1967), 276–288.

and the second deportation arrived "in the fifth month, on the seventh day of the month—which was the nineteenth year of King Nebuchadnezzar" (2 Kings 25:8; Jer. 52:12); that Ezekiel received word of the fall of Jerusalem "in the twelfth year of our exile, in the tenth month" (Ezek. 33:21); and that Jehoiachin was released from prison "in the thirty-seventh year of the exile of Jehoiachin king of Judah, in the twelfth month, on the twenty-seventh day of the month, Evil-Merodach king of Babylon, in the year that he began to reign" (2 Kings 25:27; Jer. 52:31–34).[25] There is no reason to doubt the essential accuracy of these chronological notations, but their interpretation is complicated by two problems. First, the dates provided for the two defeats of Jerusalem in 2 Kings 24:10–12; 25:8 and Jer. 52:12 (the eighth and nineteenth years of Nebuchadnezzar respectively) do not correspond, as one presumes they should, to the dates provided in Jer. 52:28–30 for the first two deportations (seventh and eighteenth years of Nebuchadnezzar). Second, we cannot be certain whether the Judean dates were calculated on the basis of a Nisan to Nisan (spring to spring) calendar as were the regnal years of the Babylonian rulers. Most scholars are inclined to believe that they were. But when one begins to compare the biblical dates with other chronological fixed points on the basis of a spring to spring calendar, a number of inconsistencies emerge. Thus some scholars strongly urge that the Judean regnal years for the period were calculated from Tishri to Tishri (autumn to autumn), which seems to remove the major difficulties.[26] In either case, Nebuchadnezzar's captain would have arrived in mid-August of 586 B.C.

The Post-Exilic Period: Ezra, Nehemiah, Haggai, and Zechariah provide specific dates for certain events in the post-Exilic period, stated in terms of the regnal years of the Persian ru'ers. Unfortunately, the dates provided cover this period only sparsely. Furthermore, the compiler of Ezra-Nehemiah appears to have telescoped some events and confused the chronological order of others.

According to Ez. 1:1 (cf. 2 Chron. 36:22; Ez. 6:3) Cyrus' decree which allowed the exiles to return to Judah was issued during his first regnal year, which began officially in March, 538 B.C. Ez. 3:1–9 informs us that returning exiles led by Jeshua and Zerubbabel built an altar in Jerusalem during the seventh month (September-October) of that year and began construction of a temple during the second

---

25. Other dated events are the beginning of the siege of Jerusalem (2 Kings 25:1; Jer. 52:4; 39:1–3; Ezek. 24:1), the city's fall (2 Kings 25:2–7; Jer. 52:5–11); and three deportations (Jer. 52:28–30).

26. Cf. esp. A. Malamat, "The Last Kings of Judah and the Fall of Jerusalem: An Historical-Chronological Study," *IEJ* 18 (1968), 137–156.

month of the next year (April-May, 537 B.C.). The next dates recorded have to do with the activity of Haggai and Zechariah during the early part of Darius' reign. We hear Haggai urging construction of the temple "in the second year of Darius the king, in the sixth month, on the first day of the month" (= August 29, 520 B.C.). Construction was begun (again?) and the temple completed on the third of Adar, Darius' sixth year (= March 12, 515 B.C.). For these and other dates recorded for the years between 520–515 B.C., see Ez. 4:24; 6:15, 19; Hag. 1:1, 15; 2:1, 10; Zech. 1:1, 7; 7:1.

Except for the activity of Ezra and Nehemiah, there is very little direct information available regarding the post-Exilic Jewish community from the time of Haggai and Zechariah until the Maccabean period.[27] The returns of Ezra and Nehemiah to Jerusalem are placed respectively in the fifth month of the seventh year of Artaxerxes (Ez. 7: 1–10), and soon after the month of Nisan of the twentieth year of Artaxerxes (Neh. 1:ff.). If the references are to Artaxerxes I in both cases, this would place Ezra's return in 458 B.C., and Nehemiah's return in 445 B.C. But several factors suggest that their careers were separated by a longer period of time and that Nehemiah actually preceded Ezra.[28] Thus many scholars place Ezra's return in the seventh year of Artaxerxes II (398 B.C.). An alternative proposal associates Ezra's career with the reign of Artaxerxes I, but emends Ez. 7:7 to read "in the *thirty*-seventh" year rather than "in the seventh year." This would place Ezra's return in 428 B.C.

We observed in the introductory chapter that historical research is not a simple matter of collecting and recounting historical facts, but involves interpretation of different kinds of evidence which often allow only tentative conclusions. Moreover, since interpretation is involved, historians working with the same sources of information often reach quite different conclusions. That this is true of historical studies of Old Testament times was illustrated in the chapters which followed. One might suppose that at least biblical historians could be expected to agree on their dates, especially since the Old Testament itself provides numerous chronological notations. But we have seen in this last chapter that the dates assigned to the persons and moments of ancient Israel belong also to the category "historical interpretation."

27. Events of the latter period are recounted in 1 Maccabees (cf. also the books of Daniel and 2 Maccabees) where they are usually dated in terms of the Seleucid era. For commentary and discussion of the chronological issues see J. R. Bartlett, *The First and Second Books of the Maccabees* (Cambridge Bible Commentary; Cambridge: University Press, 1973).
28. Cf. H. H. Rowley, "The Chronological Order of Ezra and Nehemiah," *The Servant of the Lord and Other Essays on the Old Testament* (London: Lutterworth Press, 1952), pp. 131–159.

Appendixes

Appendix I: The Archaeological Periods of Syria-Palestine and General Features of Ancient Near Eastern History

Paleolithic (Old Stone) Age: Extends from the earliest archaeological evidence of human occupation (at least as early as 300,000 years ago in Palestine, and probably much earlier) to roughly the end of the last glacial period—i.e., ca. 10,000 B.C.

Mesolithic (Middle Stone) Age: ca. 10,000–7,000 B.C.

Neolithic (New Stone) Age: ca. 7000–4000 B.C.

Chalcolithic (Copper-Stone) Age: ca. 4000–3200 B.C.

Early Bronze Age: ca. 3200–2300 B.C. This is the earliest age for which we have readable written records. In that sense it is the beginning of man's "historical period," although the available documents for the period are scarce and often fragmentary. These documents derive from Egypt's "Old Kingdom" and the Sumerian city-states of the lower Mesopotamian Valley. The Early Bronze Age witnessed the building of the pyramids and the conquests of Sargon of Akkad.

Early Bronze–Middle Bronze Transition: ca. 2300–2000 B.C. This corresponds roughly to Egypt's "First Intermediate Period." City-states, particularly Ur, continued to flourish in lower Mesopotamia. Many of the fortified cities which had been established in Syria-Palestine during the Early Bronze Age met with destruction, followed by a possible period (although this is open to challenge, see p. 54) of nomadic or semi-nomadic occupation. As we have seen, some scholars associate these supposedly less sedentary folk with the Amorites known from Mesopotamian texts, and an even larger number of scholars see this transitional age and/or the first part of the Middle Bronze Age (MB II A) as the age of the Hebrew patriarchs. In earlier archaeological terminology the EB/MB transition age was treated as two separate periods, EB IV and MB I.

Middle Bronze Age: ca. 2000–1550 B.C. The first part of this age (MB II A, ca. 2000–1800) corresponds roughly to the period of Egypt's "Middle Kingdom" and the establishment of Amorite dynasties in many of the Mesopotamian cities (e.g., Isin, Larsa, Mari, Babylon). The latter part (MB II B, ca. 1800–1650 and MB II C, ca. 1650–1550) corresponds roughly to the period of Hyksos rule in Egypt and witnessed an influx of Kassites in Mesopotamia. Once again fortified cities flourished in Syria-Palestine.

Late Bronze Age: ca. 1550–1200 B.C. This was Egypt's "Empire Age," during most of which she dominated the Palestinian city-states. Her chief competitor was the Hittite empire of Anatolia. This is also the earliest period for which we have available a significant amount of written information bearing directly upon historical circumstances in Palestine, supplied primarily by the campaign reports and the conquest lists of the pharaohs of

84

the XVIII and XIX dynasties and by the Amarna letters (see pp. 5–6). Archaeologists recognize three subdivisions within the Late Bronze Age: LB I (ca. 1550–1400), the period immediately following the expulsion of the Hyksos from Egypt; LB II A (ca. 1400–1300), the period of the Amarna tablets; and LB II B (ca. 1300–1200), the period of dynasty XIX (Sethos I, Ramses II, and Merneptah). The end of the Late Bronze Age was a turbulent time for the nations of the ancient Near East. The Hittite empire collapsed, possibly due to pressure from the "Sea Peoples," who are mentioned in the Egyptian texts and among whom were the Philistines. Egypt survived the onslaughts of the Sea Peoples, but could no longer dominate Syro-Palestinian affairs. We have noted that some biblical scholars place the Hebrew patriarchs no earlier than the Late Bronze Age. The Hebrew Exodus from Egypt belongs to this age. And Merneptah's victory stele, which dates from the very end of this age, provides the earliest non-biblical evidence of "Israel" in Palestine (see p. 7).

Iron Age: ca. 1200–333 B.C. The first part of the Iron Age witnessed the rise of local kingdoms in the ancient Near East. In addition to a number of Aramaean kingdoms in Syria and Mesopotamia, there appeared in Palestine: Edom, Moab, Ammon, a league of Philistine cities, and Israel. Syro-Palestinian affairs were dominated during the latter part of the Iron Age by a successon of larger eastern-based empires: first Assyria (beginning especially with the conquests of Tiglath-pileser III, 745–727 B.C.; ending with the fall of Nineveh in 612 B.C.), then Babylonia (612–539 B.C.), and finally Persia (539–333 B.C.). The whole of Syria-Palestine was incorporated into the Persian provincial system following the capitulation of Babylon to Cyrus in 539. The date 333 refers to Alexander the Great's victory at Issus over the Persian emperor, Darius III.

Hellenistic Period: 333–63 B.C. Following Alexander's conquests the whole Near East became strongly influenced by Hellenistic culture and was dominated by Hellenistic-oriented rulers. Palestine in particular fell first into the hands of the Ptolemaic rulers of Egypt (312–200 B.C.) and then into the hands of the Seleucid rulers of Syria (200–166 B.C.). The Maccabean rebellion against the Hellenization policies of the Seleucid rulers resulted in approximately a century of Judean independence (166–63 B.C.).

Roman Period: Jerusalem fell to Pompey in 63 B.C. By the end of the reign of Augustus Caesar (27 B.C.–A.D. 14) Rome was master of an empire which extended from the Atlantic to the Arabian and Sahara deserts.

Appendix II: Chronological Correlations between the Hebrew and Mesopotamian Kings Useful for Establishing Absolute Dates[1]

(1) The royal inscriptions of Shalmaneser III (859–824 B.C.) testify that Ahab was still on the throne of Israel during Shalmaneser's sixth year (853 B.C.) but that Jehu had ascended the throne by his fourteenth year (841 B.C.). Since we must allow for the reigns of Ahaziah and Jehoram in between, it is necessary to conclude that Ahab was nearing the end of his reign in 853 and that Jehu ascended the throne not more than a year or two before 841 (see Chapter II, p. 24).

---

1. Cf. *ANET*, pp. 266–288, 305. For items (2), (3), and (7) below see Stephanie Page, "A Stela of Adad-Nirari III and Nergal-Eres from Tell al Rimah," *Iraq* 30 (1968), pp. 139–153; Nadav Na'aman, "Sennacherib's 'Letter to God' on his Campaign to Judah," *BASOR* 214 (1974), 25–39; and D. J. Wisemann, *Chronicles of Chaldaean Kings (626–556 B.C.) in the British Museum*, pp. 32–37.

(2) Adad-nirari III (810–783 B.C.) claims in a recently discovered inscription to have received tribute from Joash of Israel. Another of his inscriptions records a campaign into the vicinity of Damascus and Philistia during his fifth year (806 B.C.), which could have occasioned this tribute. However he may have campaigned in that vicinity during other years as well.

(3) Tiglath-pileser III (745–727 B.C.) claims to have received tribute from Menahem of Israel (cf. 2 Kings 15:19–20) and Ahaz (Jehoahaz I) of Judah. Also he claims to have installed Hoshea on the throne of Israel after the overthrow of Pekah (cf. 2 Kings 15:29–31). It now seems unlikely, on the other hand, that the Azriau who appears in an annalistic fragment is to be identified with Uzziah (Azariah).

(4) 2 Kings 17:3–6 seems to imply that Shalmaneser V (727–723 B.C.) was responsible for the conquest of Samaria, although not necessarily, since "the king of Assyria" is not identified by name after verse 3. Actually, Shalmaneser's successor, Sargon II (722–705 B.C.), claims to have conquered Samaria at the beginning of his reign. Probably Shalmaneser initiated the siege of Samaria and the city fell soon after his death, the beginning of Sargon's reign.

(5) Sennacherib (705–681 B.C.) claims for his third year (701 B.C.) to have overpowered Judah and to have made Hezekiah a prisoner in Jerusalem "like a bird in a cage." 2 Kings 18:13 and Isa. 36:1 place Sennacherib's siege of Jerusalem in Hezekiah's fourteenth year.

(6) The Assyrian empire collapsed with the fall of Nineveh in 612 B.C. and Nabopolassar's expulsion of Ashur-uballit from Haran in 610/609 B.C. The Babylonian Chronicles record Ashur-uballit's unsuccessful effort to recover Haran during Nabopolassar's seventeenth year (609/608) and indicate that he was aided at that time by a large Egyptian army. This Egyptian army was probably that of Pharaoh Necho II who, on his way to the Euphrates, had defeated and killed Josiah (2 Kings 23:29). Thus Josiah's death would be dated 609/608 B.C. or slightly earlier. The battle of Carchemish, which Jer. 46:2 places in Jehoiakim's fourth year, is recorded for Nabopolassar's twenty-first year (605/604 B.C.).

(7) The Babylonian Chronicles place the first surrender of Jerusalem in Nebuchadnezzar's seventh year, the second day of the month of Adar (=March 16, 597 B.C.). 2 Kings 24:8–13 indicates that Jehoiachin had ruled only three months when the city was surrendered, and that "the king of Babylon took him prisoner in the eighth year of his reign." Since Adar was the last month of the year according to the calendar used in Babylon at the time, one is tempted to conclude that the city fell at the end of Nebuchadnezzar's seventh year but that the mopping-up operations (including the deportation of Jehoiachin) were not completed until Nebuchadnezzar's eighth year. This explanation is rendered somewhat problematic by Jer. 52:28–30, however, which gives Nebuchadnezzar's seventh year as the date of the first deportation.

(8) Jer. 32:1 indicates that Jerusalem was under siege during Zedekiah's tenth year, which it correlates with Nebuchadnezzar's eighteenth year (587/586 B.C.); and 2 Kings 25:8–21 (paralleled by Jer. 52:12–27) dates the arrival of the Babylonian captain responsible for the final destruction of Jerusalem and the second deportation "in the fifth month, on the seventh day of the month—which was the nineteenth year of King Nebuchadnezzar, king of Babylon." Again the matter is complicated by Jer. 52:28–30, which places the second deportation in Nebuchadnezzar's eighteenth year.

Appendix III: Tentative Dates for the Rulers of the Divided Kingdoms[2]

Kings of Judah	Kings of Israel			
Rehoboam	Jeroboam I	922	[924]	Roughly half a century of hostilities between the two Hebrew kingdoms (cf. esp. 1 Kings 12–16).
Abijah		915	[907]	
Asa		913	[905]	
	Nadab	901	[904]	
	Baasha	900	[903]	
	Elah	877	[886]	
	Zimri, Tibni	876	[885]	
	Omri	876	[885]	Period of the Omride dynasty. Marriage alliance between the two kingdoms (1 Kings 16–2 Kings 10).
Jehoshaphat		873	[875]	
	Ahab	869	[874]	
	Ahaziah	850	[852]	
Jehoram		849	[851]	
	Jehoram	849	[850]	
Ahaziah, Athaliah	Jehu	842	[843]	Period of severe oppression by the Aramaean kings of Damascus (2 Kings 10:32–13:25).
Jehoash		837		
	Jehoahaz	815		
	Joash	801		
Amaziah		800		
	Jeroboam II	786		A brief moment of national recovery and prosperity, especially for the northern kingdom (2 Kings 14:1–15:7).
Azariah-Uzziah		783		
Jotham (regent)		750		The smaller nations of Syria-Palestine, including Israel and Judah, are dominated by Assyria. With the fall of Samaria ca. 722, the northern kingdom ceases to exist as an independent kingdom (2 Kings 15:8–21:26).
	Zechariah	746		
	Shallum, Menahem	745		
Jotham (king)		742		
	Pekahiah	738		
	Pekah	737		
Jehoahaz I		735		
	Hoshea	732		
Fall of Samaria		722/1		
Hezekiah		715		
Manasseh		687		
Amon		642		
Josiah		640		Judah recovers her independence for a brief moment under Josiah, but is soon firmly in the hands of Babylon (2 Kings 22–24:1).
Jehoahaz II		009		
Jehoiakim		609		
Jehoiachin		598		
First Surrender of Jerusalem		598	[597]	
Zedekiah		598	[597]	
Destruction of Jerusalem		587		

2. The dates are those worked out by W. F. Albright in 1945 with suggested modifications in brackets. See pp. 80–82 and Chapter V, notes 23 and 24 for explanation and documentation.